Proud to be an
American

"Spirit of '76"
Painting by A. M. Willard, c. 1880

"Today, those sacrifices are being made by members of our Armed Forces who now defend us so far from home, and by their proud and worried families. A Commander-in-Chief sends America's sons and daughters into a battle in a foreign land only after the greatest care and a lot of prayer. We ask a lot of those who wear our uniform. We ask them to leave their loved ones, to travel great distances, to risk injury, even to be prepared to make the ultimate sacrifice of their lives. They are dedicated, they are honorable; they represent the best of our country. And we are grateful.

To all the men and women in our military—every sailor, every soldier, every airman, every coastguardsman, every Marine—I say this: Your mission is defined; your objectives are clear; your goal is just. You have my full confidence, and you will have every tool you need to carry out your duty."

President George W. Bush
November 24, 2001

Proud to be an
American

"Learn about America in a beautiful way."

Concept and Design:
Robert D. Shangle

Text by: Barbara J. Shangle
Robert D. Shangle
Paul M. Lewis
Quotations from famous American Patriots

First printing: March, 2002
ISBN: 1-58583-102-6

Published by American Products Publishing Company
Division of American Products Corporation
6750 SW 111th Avenue
Beaverton, Oregon 97008

Printed in the United States of America

Contents

Proud to be an American

From the time the first immigrant reached the shores of this country to this present day, sons and daughters have stood tall to protect the land, the values, and the manifest opportunities to which each person has rights. One should not take these attributes lightly. They are God-given Rights maintained by the stalwart devotion of the American citizen and defender of the nation.

The citizens of America are a diversity of ethnicity, having been acquired by the outstretched arms of this fledgling country's leaders that welcomed the adventuresome settler to a new land that called for establishment. Freedom and opportunity beckoned the immigrant. Freedom and opportunity beckons the immigrants today, bringing with them the ethnic cultures that create the diversity of lifestyle, language, religion and thought pattern. America is a kaleidoscope of the world's treasure—its people.

We Americans, here in the Land-of-the-Free, have more to be thankful for than any other group of people, in any other country on this planet. Many of the citizens live here without realizing the efforts put forth by the early American patriots who struggled to shape the foundation of this great nation. The good and great attributes experienced today are seldom recognized by most of the citizenry, mainly because we have been born and raised here and have lived in this country without the realization that most of the people outside our great country live a life that offers little freedom and liberty. Most of us take for granted the great freedoms we enjoy. Had it not been for the leadership of George Washington, we would be living in a much different world. Through dedication and perseverance Washington and his Continental Army successfully crossed the icy waters of the Delaware River on December 25, 1776, and surprised and defeated the Hessian mercenary forces fighting with the British. When one considers the ragtag armies that were deployed during that war, one can only marvel at the accomplishment of those soldiers and leaders of the movement.

For over 250 years people of good conscience have worked to establish an environment wherein we have a high degree of liberty and freedom. Hundreds of thousands of people have worked tirelessly for our benefit; hundreds of additional thousands have given their lives to protect the people and the nation. If you were to reflect back on the sacrifices made to protect and perpetuate the American way of life, you would experience a high degree of reverence and appreciation for those defenders. Think about the words of the Declaration of Independence and give thought to each and every word of that most important document. Give thought to those patriots of the Colonies who fought for independence against the British in the Revolutionary War; give thought to those who defended our nation during the War of 1812, the Spanish-American War, World War I, World War II, the Korean Conflict, the Vietnam War, the Gulf War, and the War in Afghanistan; give thought to all the skirmishes involving American soldiers defending freedom and liberty. Freedom and Liberty come with a price; one that must not be forgotten. We thank you.

This nation's accomplishments are unequalled. We have one of the finest education systems to be found, providing many of the leading colleges and universities in the world. Our medical centers are superior; the business acumen challenges the finest minds, establishing the United States as a world leader. Our nation and her citizens truly excel in all areas. Study our nation's history and you will be more appreciative of the accomplishments and stewardship of those who formed our country. We all have an obligation to perpetuate the vision of our Founders.

May God bless our nation and her citizens. Let us strive to be honest, good and true examples to the other peoples and nations of the world.

Our Proud Heritage

An Abbreviated/Chronological History of America

1492—October 12, Christopher Columbus sights land in America.

1513—April 12, Juan Ponce de Leon discovers Florida.

1540—Francisco Vazquez de Coronado explores southwest America.

1565—September 8. Pedro Menendez founded first European settlement in America: St. Augustine.

1579—Sir Francis Drake claims California for England.

1607—May 13. Capt. John Smith establishes Jamestown, Virginia.

1608—Spain establishes Santa Fe, New Mexico.

1620—December 21. Pilgrims land at Plymouth, Massachusetts.

1626—May 6. Peter Minuit purchases Manhattan Island from Native Americans for $24.00 worth of trinkets.

1636—Roger Williams establishes colony at Providence, Rhode Island.

1682—Robert Cavelier, Sieur de La Salle claims the Mississippi River country for France.

1683—William Penn purchases Pennsylvania lands from Native Americans.

1752—The inscription for the Liberty Bell, the biblical sentence, "Proclaim liberty throughout all the land unto all the inhabitants thereof," was chosen by the Pennsylvania Provincial Legislature. The bell was cast in England and delivered later in the year.

1754—French and Indian War begins and lasts for seven years. Battle of Fort Necessity, July 4.

George Washington, The Virginia Colonel Artist: C. W. Peale

"Colonial troops commanded by 22 year old Colonel George Washington were defeated in …[a] small stockade at the 'Great Meadow'. This opening battle of the French and Indian War began a seven year struggle between Great Britain and France for control of North America. Great Britain's success in this war helped pave the way for the American Revolution." *(www.nps.com)*

1754—May 9. The Pennsylvania Gazette published America's first newspaper cartoon, a picture of a snake cut into sections, each representing a colony, and the caption "Join or Die."

1763—February 10. The Treaty of Paris, ending the French and Indian War was signed. The French relinquished claims to Canada and all land east of the Mississippi, except New Orleans.

1764—April 5. British pass the Sugar Act placing taxes on foodstuffs, rum, molasses and lumber.

1764—April 19. British passed the Currency Act, preventing the colonies from issuing paper money as legal tender.

1765—March 22. British enact the Stamp Act to raise taxes in the American colonies to finance British armed forces in the colonies. The tax raised the major cause of the American Revolution: taxation without representation.

Patrick Henry Speech Before the House of Burgesses

1765—May 29. Patrick Henry attacked the Stamp Act in the Virginia House of Burgesses, declaring that only colonial legislatures could impose taxes on their respective colonies. Shouts of "Treason!" interrupted Henry's speech, to which he replied: "If this be treason, make the most of it."

1765—October 7-25. The Stamp Act Congress met in New York City in response to a call by the Massachusetts House of Representatives. Nine states attended and organized a united resistance to the Stamp Act, calling for a stop to importing goods from England that carried import duties.

1766—March 18. Stamp Act repealed.

1767—June 19. British enact the "Townshend Acts" to levy taxes on tea, paper, lead and glass.

1770—March 5. British fire on Bostonians in what becomes known as the Boston Massacre.

1770—April 12. British repeal Townshend Revenue Act, except for tax on tea.

1773—April 27. British passed the Tea Act which stopped all taxes on tea coming into England, but kept taxes on tea exported to the colonies. The tax almost destroyed Colonial tea merchants.

1773—December 16. Patriot Bostonians dressed as native Americans attack British commercial ships in Boston harbor and throw the cargo of tea overboard in what becomes known as "The Boston Tea Party."

1774—March 31. The first of the Intolerable Acts, also known as the Coercive Acts, was passed by the British. They were punitive acts against Massachusetts for the Boston Tea. The first act was the Boston Port Act, which closed down Boston port until payment was made for the destroyed tea of the "Boston Tea Party." The second act was the Massachusetts Government Act (May 20) which forbade public meetings unless sanctioned by the governor. The third act, the Administration of Justice Act (May 20) allowed for the transfer of British officials, when accused of capital crimes, to be sent to England or another colony for trial. The fourth act, the Quartering Act, required Massachusetts residents to house and feed British troops.

1774—December 14. The first military encounter of the American Revolution occurred. On a report of news carried by Paul Revere that the British were going to station a garrison at Portsmouth, New Hampshire, Major John Sullivan led a group of militia to Fort William and Mary, broke into the arsenal and carried off a store of arms and ammunition.

1775—January 14. British order colonial governors to forbid the importation of arms and gunpowder.

1775—March 23. Patrick Henry addresses the Virginia Convention and delivers his immortal speech against arbitrary British rule, closing with "Give me liberty, or give me death."

1775—April 18-19. William Dawes and Paul Revere ride at night to Lexington and Concord to warn that the British are on their way to confiscate colonists arms and ammunition.

"The First Blow for Liberty, Battle of Lexington"
Copy of print A. H. Ritchie, after F. O. C. Darley

1775— April 19. Colonial "Minutemen" and British clash at Lexington and Concord. The British retreat with 273 casualties, and the Americans suffer 93 casualties.

1775—May 10. Second Continental Congress meets in Philadelphia with all thirteen colonies attending.

1775—June 15. George Washington named Commander-in-Chief of the Continental American Army by the 2nd Continental Congress.

1775—June 17. Battle of Bunker Hill. The British prevail due to the colonial forces running out of ammunition.

1775—July 6. Continental Congress adopts a "Declaration of the Causes and Necessities of Taking Up Arms."

1775—August 23. British declare the Colonies in a state of rebellion and threaten to deal harshly with traitors.

1776—June 7. Richard Henry Lee, of Virginia, in the Continental Congress makes a motion "that these united colonies are and of right ought to be free and independent states." A resolution on the motion is adopted on July 2.

1776—June 11. Congress appoints committee chaired by Thomas Jefferson to draft a declaration of independence.

Paul Revere's Ride April 18-19, 1775

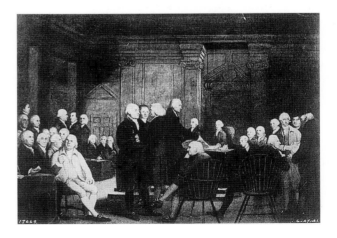

The Second Continental Congress Voting Independence

1776—June 28. Jefferson's draft of the Declaration of Independence, with changes proposed by Franklin and Adams is submitted to Congress.

1776—June 29. Virginia, the first colony to change its form of government pursuant to the resolution adopted by Congress on May 10, adopts a new constitution for an independent Commonwealth of Virginia.

1776—July 2. Twelve of the thirteen delegations in Congress (New York abstained) vote for the principle of independence.

1776—July 4. Congress adopts the Jefferson draft of the Declaration of Independence.

1776—August 27. British forces defeat the Americans in the Battle of Long Island.

1776—September 22. Nathan Hale executed by the British in New York City for spying. Before he was hanged he made the statement, "I only regret that I have but one life to lose for my country."

1777—September 11. Washington's forces defeated by the British at Brandywine, Pennsylvania.

1777—September 19. The Continental Congress flees Philadelphia as the British forces approach.

1777—September 26. Philadelphia is occupied by the British.

1777—October 4. Washington's forces repulsed by the British at Germantown near Philadelphia.

1777—October 7. Americans defeat the British in the Second Battle of Bemis Heights, near Saratoga, New York.

1777—October 17. American forces defeat the British at Saratoga, New York.

1777—November 15. Continental Congress adopts the Articles of Confederation.

Washington Crossing the Delaware, a painting by Emanuel Leutze, dated 1851, commemorates the Battle of Trenton, December 25-26, 1776

1776—December 25-26. Washington's forces cross the Delaware River and attack the Hessians at Trenton, defeating them and taking nearly 1,000 prisoners in an early morning surprise attack.

1777—January 3. Washington's forces defeat the British at Princeton. An early morning attack, which had worked at Trenton the previous week, worked again for the Continental Army.

1777—June 14. Continental Congress selects the "Stars and Stripes" as the official American flag.

1777—July 6. British recapture Fort Ticonderoga.

1777—August 16. Americans defeat the British at Bennington, Vermont. Over 200 British soldiers were killed and over 600 were taken prisoner.

1777—December 17. Washington takes his forces to Valley Forge for a winter camp.

"George Washington and a Committee of Congress at Valley Forge" Artist: W. H. Powell

1778—February 6. France recognizes the independence of the colonials and joins the war against the British.

1778—June 28. British are defeated by Washington's forces at Monmouth, New Jersey, after several battle reversals.

1778—August 16. American forces defeated by the British at the battle of Camden in South Carolina.

1779—September 23. John Paul Jones, commanding the *Bonhomme Richard* defeats and captures the *Serapis*, a British man-of-war. It was in this battle that Jones when asked if he would surrender, replies, "I have not yet begun to fight."

1780—August 16. American forces are defeated by the British at the Battle of Camden in South Carolina.

1781—October 19. Cornwallis surrenders to Washington at Yorktown.

"Surrender of Cornwallis" by Artist John Trumbull

1782—November 30. Americans and British sign preliminary articles of peace in Paris.

1783—September 3. Britain and the United States sign a peace treaty ending the war for independence of the thirteen colonies.

1783—November 3. Washington orders the disbanding of the army.

1787—May 25. Constitutional Convention convenes in Philadelphia. George Washington presides.

1787—September 17. The Constitution is adopted by the Convention.

1788—June 21. The Constitution is ratified by the ninth state, New Hampshire, bringing to effect a legal adoption.

1789—February 4. George Washington chosen first President of the United States of America.

1789— March 4. The Constitution declared in effect.

1791—December 15. The Bill of Rights becomes effective.

1792—December 5. Washington elected to second term as president.

1796—September 19. Washington leaves office, and in his farewell address gives strong warnings against permanent alliances with foreign powers, big public debt, a large military establishment, and devices of "small, artful, enterprising minority" to control or change government.

1796—December. John Adams elected second President of the United States.

1801—March 4. Thomas Jefferson sworn in as third President of the United States.

1803—December 20. Louisiana Purchase completed for approximately $15,000,000 doubling the land area of the United States.

1804—May 4. Lewis and Clark Expedition leaves St. Louis to explore the "west," returning to St. Louis September 23, 1806.

1808—December 7. James Madison elected fourth President of the United States.

1812—June 18. Congress declares war on England. War of 1812.

1814—September 13-14. British fleet bombards Fort McHenry, and fail. Francis Scott Key writes the words to "The Star Spangled Banner," which is a record of Key's experience of the Fort McHenry bombardment.

1815—January 8. American forces under command of General Andrew Jackson defeat the British in the Battle of New Orleans. The British had 2,000-plus casualties, the Americans had about 70.

1823—December 2. The Monroe Doctrine proclaimed.

1826—July 4. Thomas Jefferson and John Adams die, one of the most remarkable coincidences in American history.

1835—November. Texas secedes from Mexico and Sam Houston commands a Texas army.

1836—March 6. Texans besieged by the Mexican army at the Alamo with the entire garrison being killed.

1842—Settlement of the Oregon Territory begins.

1861—Civil War begins.

1862—Emancipation Proclamation issued by President Lincoln.

1865—April 9. General Robert E. Lee of the Confederacy surrenders to Union General, Ulysses S. Grant at Appomattax Court House, ending the Civil War.

1886—France gifts to the United States the Statue of Liberty.

1898—April 25. War is declared with Spain: the Spanish-American War. Spain surrenders August 12.

1917—April 6. The United States enters World War I.

1918—November 11. World War I ends.

1941—December 8. The United States enters World War II against Japan.

1941—December 11. Germany and Italy declare war on the United States. The U. S. Congress acknowledges a state of war.

1945—May 8. V-E Day. Victory in Europe is declared.

1945—August 15. V-J Day. Victory in Japan is declared.

1950—June 27-30. President Harry Truman approves use of Air Force, Navy and military grounds forces in the Korean conflict.

1953—July 27. Korean conflict fighting ends.

1964—August 7. Tonkin Resolution by Congress authorizes military action in Vietnam.

1973—January 22. Vietnam Peace Agreement signed in Paris by United States, North and South Vietnam and the Vietcong.

1991—January 16. First shots of the Gulf War between the United States and Iraq.

1991—February 28. Cease-fire declared to end the Gulf War.

2001—September 11. The greatest single disaster to befall the American people occurs with the destruction of the World Trade Center in New York City and a partial destruction to the Pentagon in Arlington, Virginia, near Washington, D.C.

The Birthplace of the Nation

Carpenters' Hall, Independence National Historical Park, Philadelphia, Pennsylvania

A building long remembered as the "Birthplace of a Nation" is Carpenters' Hall, completed in 1774, just in time to house one of the most important meetings in America's history. The National Park Service best explains: "When the First Continental Congress met to decide ways of recovering certain colonial rights and liberties violated by various acts of the British government, Philadelphia was the logical choice for the meeting. The principal city of the Colonies, it offered not only all the amenities the delegates needed but also a central location between North and South, a major consideration in an era of slow, tedious, and sometimes dangerous travel…. The Congress convened at Carpenters' Hall in September 1774 and addressed a declaration of rights and grievances to King George III. The delegates also agreed to boycott English goods and resolved that, unless their grievances were redressed, a second Congress should assemble the following spring. England did nothing to satisfy American complaints…. The Carpenters' Company was organized to share information about the art of building, determine the value of completed work, hone architectural skills, and help indigent craftsmen…. [It is] the oldest trade guild in the country." *(www.ushistory.org)* Carpenters' Hall served as the headquarters for the First Bank of the United States in 1791. A nostalgic visit to the Hall allows a step back into history, with the ability to step "in their footsteps," view original furniture, and visit with an informative guide. The Carpenters' Company still own and operate the hall, a vital part of American heritage. *Photo by James Blank*

The Declaration of Independence, 4, July 1776, A painting by John Trumbull (Trumbull served as Washington's aide-de-camp in the Continental Army.)

"The Declaration of Independence," one of the eight paintings hanging in the Rotunda of the nation's Capitol in Washington, D. C., depicts a monumental event in our history that took place in Independence Hall, Philadelphia, July 4, 1776. The fifty-six men who signed the Declaration, all members of the Continental Congress, risked death to tell the world that "for the support of this Declaration…we mutally pledge to each other our Lives, our Fortunes, and our sacred Honor."

The History of the Declaration of Independence

Nations come into being in many ways. Military rebellion, civil strife, acts of heroism, acts of treachery, a thousand greater and lesser clashes between defenders of the old order and supporters of the new—all these occurrences and more have marked the emergences of new nations, large and small. The birth of our own nation included them all. That birth was unique, not only in the immensity of its later impact on the course of world history and the growth of democracy, but also because so many of the threads in our national history run back through time to come together in one place, in one time, and in one document: the Declaration of Independence.

The clearest call for independence up to the summer of 1776 came in Philadelphia on June 7. On that date in session in the Pennsylvania State House (later Independence Hall), the Continental Congress heard Richard Henry Lee of Virginia read his resolution beginning: "Resolved: That these United Colonies are, and of right ought to be, free and independent States, that they are absolved from all allegiance to the British Crown, and that all political connection between them and the State of Great Britain is, and ought to be, totally dissolved."

The Lee Resolution was an expression of what was already beginning to happen throughout the colonies. When the Second Continental Congress, which was essentially the government of the United States from 1775 to 1788, first met in May 1775, King George III had not replied to the petition for redress of grievances that had been sent by the First Continental Congress. The Congress gradually took on the responsibilities of a national government. In June 1775 the Congress established the Continental Army as well as a continental currency. By the end of July of that year, it created a post office for the "United Colonies."

In August 1775 a royal proclamation declared that the King's American subjects were "engaged in open and avowed rebellion." Later that year, Parliament passed the American Prohibitory Act, which made all American vessels and cargoes forfeit to the Crown. And in May 1776 the Congress learned that the King had negotiated treaties with German states to hire mercenaries to fight in America. The weight of these actions combined to convince many Americans that the mother country was treating the colonies as a foreign entity.

One by one, the Continental Congress continued to cut the colonies' ties to Britain. The Privateering Resolution, passed in March 1776, allowed the colonists "to fit out armed vessels to cruize [sic] on the enemies of these United Colonies." On April 6, 1776, American ports were opened to commerce with other nations, an action that severed the economic ties fostered by the Navigation Acts. A "Resolution for the Formation of Local Governments" was passed on May 10, 1776.

At the same time, more of the colonists themselves were becoming convinced of the inevitability of independence. Thomas Paine's *Common Sense*, published in January 1776, was sold by the thousands. By the middle of May 1776, eight colonies had decided that they would support independence. On May 15, 1776, the Virginia Convention passed a resolution that "the delegates appointed to represent this colony in General Congress be instructed to propose to that respectable body to declare the United Colonies free and independent states."

It was in keeping with these instructions that Richard Henry Lee, on June 7, 1776, presented his resolution. There were still some delegates, however, including those bound by earlier instructions, who wished to pursue the path of reconciliation with Britain. On June 11 consideration of the Lee Resolution was postponed by a vote of seven colonies to five, with New York abstaining. Congress then recessed for three weeks. The tone of the debate indicated that at the end of that time the Lee Resolution would be adopted. Before Congress recessed, therefore, a Committee of Five was appointed to draft a statement presenting to the world the colonies' case for independence.

The committee consisted of two New England men, John Adams of Massachusetts and Roger Sherman of Connecticut; two men from the Middle Colonies, Benjamin Franklin of Pennsylvania and Robert R. Livingston of New York; and one Southerner, Thomas Jefferson of Virginia. In 1823 Jefferson wrote that the other members of the committee "unanimously pressed on myself alone to undertake the draught [sic]. I consented; I drew it; but before I reported it to the committee I communicated it separately to Dr. Franklin and Mr. Adams requesting their corrections…I then wrote a fair copy, reported it to the committee, and from them, unaltered to the Congress."

Jefferson's account reflects three stages in the life of the Declaration: the document originally written by Jefferson; the changes to that document made by Franklin and Adams, resulting in the version that was submitted by the Committee of Five to the Congress; and the version that was eventually adopted.

On July 1, 1776, Congress reconvened. The following day, the Lee Resolution for independence was adopted by 12 of the 13 colonies, New York not voting. Immediately afterward, the Congress began to consider the Declaration. Adams and Franklin had made only a few changes before the committee submitted the document. The discussion in Congress resulted in some alterations and deletions, but the basic document remained Jefferson's. The process of revision continued through all of July 3 and into the late afternoon of July 4. Then, at last, church bells rang out over Philadelphia; the Declaration had been officially adopted.

Information from the National Archives and Records Administration

Declaration of Independence

In Congress, July 4, 1776

The unanimous Declaration of the thirteen united States of America

When in the Course of human events, it becomes necessary for one people to dissolve the political bands which have connected them with another, and to assume among the powers of the earth, the separate and equal station to which the Laws of Nature and of Nature's God entitle the, a decent respect to the opinions of mankind requires that they should declare the causes which impel them to the separation.   We hold these truths to be self-evident, that all men are created equal, that they are endowed by their Creator with certain unalienable Rights, that among these are Life, Liberty and the pursuit of Happiness. That to secure these rights, Governments are instituted among Men, deriving their just powers from the consent of the governed. That whenever any Form of Government becomes destructive of these ends, it is the Right of the People to alter or to abolish it, and to institute new Government, laying its foundation on such principles and organizing its powers in such form, as to them shall seem most likely to effect their Safety and Happiness. Prudence, indeed, will dictate that Governments long established should not be changed for light and transient causes; and accordingly all experience hath shewn, that mankind are more disposed to suffer, while evils are sufferable, than to right themselves by abolishing the forms to which they are accustomed. But when a long train of abuses and usurpations, pursuing invariable the same Object, evinces a design to reduce them under absolute Despotism, it is their right, it is their duty, to throw off such Government, and to provide new Guards for their future security. Such has been the patient sufferance of these Colonies; and such is now the necessity which constrains them to alter their former Systems of Government. The history of the present King of Great Britain is a history of repeated injuries and usurpations, all having in direct object the establishment of an absolute Tyranny over these States. To prove this, let Facts be submitted to a candid world.   He has refused his Assent to Laws, the most wholesome and necessary for public good. He has forbidden his Governors to pass laws of immediate and pressing importance, unless suspended in their operation till his Assent should be obtained; and when so suspended, he has utterly neglected to attend to them.   He has refused to pass other Laws for the accommodation of large districts of people, unless those people would relinquish the right of Representation in the Legislature, a right inestimable to them and formidable to tyrants only.   He has called together legislative bodies at places unusual, uncomfortable, and distant from the depository of their public Records, for the sole purpose of fatiguing them into compliance with his measures.   He has dissolved Representative Houses repeatedly, for opposing with manly firmness his invasions on the rights of the people.   He has refused for a long time, after such dissolutions, to cause others to be elected; whereby the Legislative powers, incapable of Annihilation, have returned to the People at large for their exercise; the State remaining in the meantime exposed to all the dangers of invasion from without, and convulsions within.   He has endeavoured to prevent the population of these States; for that purpose obstructing the Laws of Naturalization of Foreigners; refusing to pass others to encourage their migrations hither, and raising the conditions of new Appropriations of Lands.
He has obstructed the Administration of Justice, by refusing his Assent to Laws for establishing Judiciary powers. He has made Judges dependent on his Will alone, for the tenure of their offices, and the amount and payment of their salaries.   He has erected a multitude of New Offices, and sent hither swarms of Officers to harass our people, and eat out their substance.   He has kept among us in times of peace, Standing Armies without the Consent of our legislatures.   He has affected to render the Military independent of and superior to the Civil power.   He has combined with others to subject us to a jurisdiction foreign to our constitution, and unacknowledged by our laws; giving his Assent to their Acts of pretended Legislation: For quartering large bodies of armed troops among us: For protecting them, by a mock Trial, from punishment for any Murders which they should commit on the Inhabitants of these States: For cutting off our Trade with all parts of the world: For imposing Taxes on us without our Consent: For depriving us in many cases, of the benefits of Trial by Jury: For transporting us beyond Seas to be tried for pretended offences: For abolishing the free System of English Laws in a neighbouring Province, establishing therein an Arbitrary government, and enlarging its Boundaries so as to render it at once an example and fit instrument for introducing the same absolute rule into these Colonies: for taking away our Charters, abolishing our most valuable Laws, and altering fundamentally the Forms of our Governments: For suspending our own Legislatures and declaring themselves invested with power to legislate for us in all cases whatsoever.   He has abdicated Government here, by declaring us out of His Protection and waging War against us.   He has plundered our seas, ravaged our Coasts, burnt our towns, and destroyed the lives of our people.   He is at this time transporting large Armies of foreign Mercenaries to complete the works of death, desolation and tyranny, already begun with circumstances of Cruelty & perfidy scarcely paralleled in the most barbarous ages, and totally unworthy the Head of a civilized nation.   He has constrained our fellow Citizens taken Captive on the high Seas to bear Arms against their Country, to become the executioners of their friends and Brethren, or to fall themselves by their Hands.
He has excited domestic insurrections amongst us, and has endeavoured to bring on the inhabitants of our frontiers, the merciless Indian Savages, whose known rule of warfare, is an undistinguished destruction of all ages, sexes and conditions. In every stage of these Oppressions We have Petitioned for Redress in the most humble terms. Our repeated Petitions have been answered only by repeated injury. A Prince, whose character is thus marked by every act which may define a Tyrant, is unfit to be the ruler of a free people. Nor have We been wanting in attention to our Brittish brethren. We have warned them from time to time of attempts by their legislature to extend an unwarrantable jurisdiction over us. We have reminded them of the circumstances of our emigration and settlement here. We have appealed to their native justice and magnanimity, and we have conjured them by the ties of our common kindred to disavow these usurpations, which, would inevitably interrupt our connections and correspondence. They too have been deaf to the voice of justice and of consanguinity. We must, therefore, acquiesce in the necessity which denounces our Separation, and hold them, as we hold the rest of mankind, Enemies in War, in Peace Friends.

WE, THEREFORE, the Representatives of the UNITED STATES of AMERICA, in General Congress, Assembled, appealing to the Supreme Judge of the world for the rectitude of our intentions, do, in the Name, and by Authority of the good People of these Colonies, solemnly publish and declare, That these United Colonies are, and of Right ought to be, FREE AND INDEPENDENT STATES; that they are Absolved from all Allegiance to the British Crown, and that all political connection between them and the State of Great Britain, is and ought to be totally dissolved; and that as Free and Independent States, they have full Power to levy War, conclude Peace, contract Alliances, establish Commerce, and to do all other Acts and Things which INDEPENDENT States may of right do. AND for the support of this Declaration, with a firm reliance on the protection of Divine Providence, we mutually pledge to each other our Lives, our Fortunes, and our sacred Honor.

Scene at the Signing of the Constitution, Artist Howard Chandler Christy

"Scene at the Signing of the Constitution" was commissioned by Congress in 1940 for the east stairway in the House of Representatives wing in the Capitol. The twenty feet by thirty feet canvas, largest in the Capitol, is remarkable for its historic detail and its patriotic inspiration. Eleven years after independence from England was declared, the leaders of the new nation met in Independence Hall, September 17, 1787, to place their names on this modern document of freedom. Well known likenesses of George Washington, Benjamin Franklin, Alexander Hamilton, and James Madison are easily recognized.

About the Constitution of the United States

The governing power of the United States of America is embodied in the Constitution, adopted September 17, 1787. As simple as this may sound, it is far from a quickly composed instrument. Its strength encompasses efforts of powerful, intellectual minds who endeavored to create a written instrument that provides self-government, independence of mind and thought, and the right of man to move forward in a free, unencumbered way of life. Based on the ideal of Federalism (preferring a centralized national government), the authors of the United States Constitution protected against "power by few" by dividing authority into three branches of government: the executive, the judicial, and the legislative. Employing the "checks and balances" system, each branch monitors the activities of the other two branches, striving to keep a balance among the three.

With the knowledge acquired from previous governmental instruments and from the actions of the people, the Constitutional framers understood the ramifications of the written word. The Magna Carta, adopted by the British Monarchy and ruling Barons in 1215, provided for the beginning of protection of civil liberties. In 1620 the "Separationists," more commonly identified today as the Pilgrims, joined together on the ship *Mayflower* and sailed to the New World, seeking freedom from religious persecution. Upon their arrival and before disembarking the ship, the Pilgrims composed an instrument known as The Mayflower Compact, designed for self-government that would allow the banding together "to enact, constitute and frame such just and equal Laws, Ordinances, Acts, Constitutions and Offices" needed for the convenience of governing.

As immigrants established homes, created businesses, churches, and a way of life in the New World, the desire for self preservation was strong. As generations of people sprang forth, ties to the Mother Country began to fade for many. The independent strength of the New World citizen sent out deep roots that developed societal structure and established new heritage conviction. Many felt the need for "independence" from British rule, providing the impetus for the American Revolution.

In June of 1776 Thomas Jefferson was appointed by the Continental Congress to draft a resolution with the expressed intent of declaring the Colonies "free and independent states...absolved from allegiance to the British Crown." On July 2, 1776, after many hours and over many days of revision by Jefferson and members of Congress, the Declaration of Independence was completed, and on July 4, 1776, the Declaration was adopted by Congress.

In January, 1777, Congress began the chore of composing The Articles of Confederation, a document used for the purpose of unification of rule by the original thirteen colonies, while maintaining state freedom and for its citizens. The voluminous document containing thirteen articles was finally adopted November 15, 1777. Not taken lightly by any of the Colonies, it was a four-year process before all thirteen Colonies ratified the Articles of Confederation, becoming in force March 1, 1781.

Following the victory by the Patriots over the British, Congress realized the inadequacy of the Articles of Confederation and the need for a stronger federal union. On February 12, 1787, the monumental task of revising the Articles was undertaken. A three-branch governmental plan was created: Executive (Presidential), Judicial (Supreme Court), and Legislative (Congress). The Legislative allowed for two chambers of control: The Senate or Upper House having two members per state with one vote each, and the House of Representatives or Lower House having its members determined by the populace census of each state. Seven months later, on September 17, 1787, the Constitution of the United States was signed and established by Congress.

The strength of the Constitution has been tested over the many years, accepting challenges by such confrontations as the Civil War, a grueling threat to the Federal Union. By its flexibility and inherent wisdom, the Constitution has provided the foundation of guidance to govern the citizens of the United States of America for well over 200 years.

Independence Hall, Philadelphia, Pennsylvania Considered by many to be the most important building in American history, the Second Continental Congress met here from 1775 to 1783 with a gathering of men who designed and adopted the Declaration of Independence, the Articles of Confederation, and the signing of the United States Constitution. *Photo by James Blank*

The United States Flag
Symbol of our Freedom

"The flag…is a visible symbol of the ideal aspirations of the American people. It is the one focus in which all unite in reverential devotion. We differ in religion; we differ in politics; we engage in disputes as to the true meaning of the Constitution, and even challenge the wisdom of some of its provisions; we inject self-interest and cupidity into most of the ordinary transactions of daily life, but through the sanctifying folds of the flag, the collective intelligence of the nation rises superior to the wisdom of its parts, and thus ensures the perpetuity of the Republic."—Major General Arthur MacArthur

The story of the origin of our National flag parallels the story of the origin of our country. As our country received its birthright from the peoples of many lands who were gathered on these shores to found a new nation, so did the pattern of the Stars and Stripes rise from several origins back in the mists of antiquity to become emblazoned on the standards of our infant Republic.

The first flag of the colonists to have any resemblance to the present Stars and Stripes was the Grand Union flag, sometimes referred to as the "Congress Colors." It consisted of thirteen stripes, alternately red and white, representing the Thirteen Colonies, with a blue field in the upper left hand corner bearing the crosses of St. George and St. Andrew, signifying union with the mother country. This banner was first flown by the ships of the Colonial Fleet in the Delaware River in December, 1775.

Continental Congress passed a resolution that established the Stars and Stripes on June 14, 1777, but did not specify the arrangement of the thirteen stars on the blue union, except to say that they should represent a new constellation. As a consequence we find a variety of forms. The first Army flag, popularly known as the Betsy Ross flag, had them arranged in a circle, based on the idea that no colony should take precedence.

The Resolution of June 14, 1777, establishing the Stars and Stripes has an interesting history. After the Declaration of Independence, colonial vessels were putting to sea to hamper enemy communications and prey on British commerce. Many of them flew the flags of the particular Colonies to which they belonged. It was necessary to provide an authorized national flag under which they could sail, for England considered armed vessels without such a flag as pirate ships and hanged their crews when they captured them. So the Marine Committee of the Second Continental Congress presented the Resolution, which was on the subject of the Navy.

General Washington, when the Star-Spangled Banner was first flown by the Continental Army, is said to have described its symbolism as follows: "We take the stars from heaven, the red from our mother country, separating it by white stripes, thus showing that we have separated from her, and the white stripes shall go down to posterity representing liberty."

Realizing that the flag would become unwieldy with a stripe for each new State, Captain Samuel C. Reid, USN, suggested to Congress that the stripes remain thirteen in number to represent the Thirteen Colonies, and that a star be added to the blue field for each new State coming into the Union. A law of April 4, 1818, that resulted requires that a star be added for each new State on the 4th of July after its admission.

Thus the Stars and Stripes came into being; born amid the strife of battle, it became the standard around which a free people struggled to found a great nation. Its spirit is fervently expressed in the words of Thomas Jefferson:

"I swear, before the altar of God, eternal hostility to every form of tyranny over the mind of man."

Information quoted from House Document No. 395, 87th Congress, 2d Session

President George W. Bush

43rd President of the United States
Inaugural Address
January 20, 2001

President Clinton, distinguished guests and my fellow citizens, the peaceful transfer of authority is rare in history, yet common in our country. With a simple oath, we affirm old traditons and make new beginnings.

As I begin, I thank President Clinton for his service to our nation. And I thank Vice President Gore for a contest conducted with spirit and ended with grace.

I am honored and humbled to stand here, where so many of America's leaders have come before me, and so many will follow.

We have a place, all of us, in a long story—a story we continue, but whose end we will not see. It is the story of a new world that became a friend and liberator of the old, a story of a slave-holding society that became a servant of freedom, the story of a power that went into the world to protect but not possess, to defend but not to conquer.

It is the American story—a story of flawed and fallible people, united across the generations by grand and enduring ideals.

The grandest of these ideals is an unfolding American promise that everyone belongs, that everyone deserves a chance, that no insignificant person was ever born.

Americans are called to enact this promise in our lives and in our laws. And though our nation has sometimes halted, and sometimes delayed, we must follow no other course.

Through much of the last century, America's faith in freedom and democracy was a rock in a raging sea. Now it is a seed upon the wind, taking root in many nations.

Our democratic faith is more than the creed of our country, it is the inborn hope of our humanity, an ideal we carry but do not own, a trust we bear and pass along. And even after nearly 225 years, we have a long way yet to travel.

While many of our citizens prosper, others doubt the promise, even the justice, of our own country. The ambitions of some Americans are limited by failing schools and hidden prejudice and the circumstances of their birth. And sometimes our differences run so deep, it seems we share a continent, but not a country.

We do not accept this, and we will not allow it. Our unity, our union, is the serious work of leaders and citizens in every generation. And this is my solemn pledge: I will work to build a single nation of justice and opportunity.

I know this is in our reach because we are guided by a power larger than ourselves who creates us equal in His image.

And we are confident in principles that unite and lead us onward.

America has never been united by blood or birth or soil. We are bound by ideals that move us beyond our backgrounds, lift us above our interest and teach us what it means to be citizens. Every child must be taught these principles. Every citizen must uphold them. And every immigrant, by embracing these ideals, makes our country more, not less, American.

Today, we affirm a new commitment to live out our nation's promise through civility, courage, compassion and character.

America, at its best, matches a commitment to principle with a concern for civility. A civil society demands from each of us good will and respect, fair dealing and forgiveness.

Some seem to believe that our politics can afford to be petty because, in a time of peace, the stakes of our debates appear small.

Continued on page 85

The Pledge of Allegiance

I pledge allegiance to the flag
of the United States of America
and to the Republic for which it stands,
one Nation under God,
indivisible,
with liberty and justice for all.

The Pledge was written by Francis Bellamy of Rome, New York, and published in "The Youth's Companion" on September 8, 1882. It was June 22, 1942, that Congress officially recognized the Pledge of Allegiance. Small word changes have occurred twice to the Pledge, on June 14, 1923 and June 14, 1954, National Flag Day in the United States of America.

The American's Creed

The American's Creed defines what it means to be American, both the need for FAITH in who and what we are as a Nation, and the RESPONSIBILITY we all have to love and respect our Nation and its Flag. Its message is appropriate for each generation of American, but becomes even more meaningful when we understand the historical context of its origin…written during a time of conflict and turmoil at home and abroad.

I believe in the United States of America as a government of the people, by the people, for the people; whose just powers are derived from the consent of the governed; a democracy in a republic; a sovereign Nation of many sovereign States; a perfect union, one and inseparable, established upon those principles of freedom, equality, justice and humanity for which American patriots sacrificed their lives and fortunes.

I therefore believe it is my duty to my country to love it, to support its Consitution, to obey its laws, to respect its flag, and to defend it against all enemies.

William Tyler Page, April 3, 1918

America's involvement in World War I was a difficult and divisive issue for our Nation. President Wilson had struggled for three years since the outbreak of hostilities in August 1914 to maintain a position of American neutrality towards the European conflict. This effort to distance our Nation from European affairs was disturbed on May 7, 1915, when a German U-boat sank the unarmed British liner Lusitania, killing more than 1,000 people, including 128 Americans.

By 1917 it was becoming increasingly apparent that American neutrality could no longer be maintained. President Wilson went before Congress to request a Declaration of War with these words:

"The world must be made safe for democracy. It is a fearful thing to lead this great peaceful people into war, the most terrible of wars. But the right is more precious than the peace, and we shall fight for the things that we have always carried nearest our hearts…for democracy…for the rights and liberties of small nations, for a universal dominion of right by such a concert of free peoples as shall bring peace and safety to all nations and make the world itself at last free."

President Wilson's view of the United States as the stalwart of world democracy wasn't shared by everyone, however. Six of the 96 U. S. Senators voted against the declaration of war. The House of Representatives passed the resolution April 6, 1917, but only after 13 hours of emotional and heated debate. Fifty congressional votes were cast against the declaration.

By midsummer Gen. John J. Pershing's American Expeditionary Force was landing in Europe. Congress' new program of conscription under the Selective Service Act was mandating registration for military service by every American man between the ages of 21 and 30 years of age. Not since the Civil War had an issue arisen to so divide the country. Citizens began to protest American involvement in "Europe's troubles" and the forced recruitment of soldiers in the Selective Service Act. By the summer of 1918 the war in Europe had forced the Government to take control of industry, railroads, and food and fuel production. Taxes were raised to fund the war, postal rates went up, and censorship of some mail was being officially conducted. In May Congress passed the Sedition Act which allowed war and draft protesters to be jailed. More than 2,000 Americans were already behind bars for interfering with the draft, including one former United States Congressman.

In the midst of all this domestic turmoil and dissension, a nationwide essay contest was held to develop an American's Creed. The winning entry was submitted by William Tyler Page of Friendship Heights, Maryland. Mr. Page was a descendent of President John Tyler and former Congressman John Page who served in the House of Representatives from 1789-1797. William Tyler Page himself had also served in Congress as a Congressional Page in 1881. His winning essay established the American's Creed.

Information by C. Douglas Sterner, www.homeofheroes.com

Obverse Side of the Great Seal

The Reverse Side of the Great Seal

The Great Seal of the United States of America

On July 4, 1776, the Continental Congress appointed a committee consisting of Benjamin Franklin, John Adams and Thomas Jefferson "to bring in a device for a seal of the United States of America." After many delays, a verbal description of a design by William Barton was final, approved by Congress on June 20, 1782. The seal shows an American bald eagle with a ribbon in its mouth bearing the words *E pluribus unum* (One out of many). In its talons are the arrows of war and an olive branch of peace. On the reverse side it shows an unfinished pyramis with an eye (the eye of Providence) above it.

The Great Seal was first used on September 16, 1782, on a document granting General George Washington authority to consult with the British about prisoner exchanges. On September 15, 1789, Congress declared that the Great Seal was to be the official seal of the United States, and that it was to be kept in custody of the Secretary of State. Since then six dies of the Seal have been officially cut and used. The reverse side of the Great Seal has never been cut.

The Bald Eagle
An American Symbol

The Eagle became the National Emblem of the United States on June 20, 1782, when the Great Seal of the United States was adopted to represent the new country. The wide-spread wings of the eagle facing front has on his breast a shield with thirteen perpendicular red-and-white stripes, surmounted by a blue field with thirteen stars. In his right talon the eagle holds an olive branch and in his left talon he holds a bundle of thirteen arrows. A scroll held in his beak is inscribed with the words *"E Pluribus Unum,"* meaning, " one made out of many." These words were chosen by Benjamin Franklin, Thomas Jefferson and John Adams.

Living as he does on the tops of lofty mountains amid the solitary grandeur of nature, the eagle has come to represent freedom to many Americans. A story relates an incident during an early morning battle during the American Revolution when the intense noise awoke the sleeping eagles on the nearby heights and they flew from their nests circling about over the heads of the fighting men, all the while giving vent to their raucous cries. The patriots exclaimed, "They are shrieking for Freedom."

The eagle appears on the Seals of many of our states and on most of our gold and silver coins. The eagle is incorporated into patriot efforts and materials.

Statue of Liberty National Monument

"Located in New York Harbor, the Statue of Liberty was a gift of international friendship from the people of France to the people of the United States and is one of the most universal symbols of political freedom and democracy. The Statue of Liberty was dedicated on October 28, 1886 and was designated a National Monument on October 15, 1924. The Statue was extensively restored in time for her spectacular centennial on July 4, 1986."

Some interesting facts about the statue include: the statue height from the base of the statue to the torch is 151 feet 1 inch and from the ground to the tip of the torch is 305 feet 1 inch. The length of the hand is 16 feet 1 inch, with the index finger measuring 8 feet. The statue's head is 10 feet thick; each eye measures 2 feet 6 inches across; and the length of the nose is 4 feet 6 inches. The right arm measures a distance of 42 feet and her waist measures 35 feet thick. The mouth measures 3 feet.

The design of the statue's crown has significant meaning: each of the twenty-five windows "symbolize gemstones found on the earth and the heaven's rays shining over the world;" The seven spoking rays "represent the seven seas and continents of the world." The statue's left hand holds a tablet that reads in Roman Numeral letters "July 4, 1776."

Information provided by the National Park Service

In God We Trust

History of the Motto
"In God We Trust"

The United States National Motto

The motto IN GOD WE TRUST was placed on United States coins largely because of the increased religious sentiment existing during the Civil War. Secretary of the Treasury Salmon P. Chase received many appeals from devout persons throughout the country, urging that the United States recognize the Deity on United States coins. From Treasury Department records, it appears that the first such appeal came in a letter dated November 13, 1861. It was written to Secretary Chase by Rev. M. R. Watkinson, Minister of the Gospel from Ridleyville, Pennsylvania, and read:

Dear Sir: You are about to submit your annual report to the Congress respecting the affairs of the national finances.

One fact touching our currency has hitherto been seriously overlooked. I mean the recognition of the Almighty God in some form on our coins.

You are probably a Christian. What if our Republic were not shattered beyond reconstruction? Would not the antiquaries of succeeding centuries rightly reason from our past that we were a heathen nation? What I propose is that instead of the goddess of liberty we shall have next inside the 13 stars a ring inscribed with the words PERPETUAL UNION; within the ring the allseeing eye, crowned with a halo; beneath this eye the American flag, bearing in its field stars equal to the number of the States united; in the folds of the bars the words GOD, LIBERTY, LAW.

This would make a beautiful coin, to which no possible citizen could object. This would relieve us from the ignominy of heathenism. This would place us openly under the Divine protection we have personally claimed. From my heart I have felt our national shame in disowning God as not the least of our present national disasters.

To you first I address a subject that must be agitated.

As a result, Secretary Chase instructed James Pollock, Director of the Mint at Philadelphia, to prepare a motto, in a letter dated November 20, 1861:

Dear Sir: No nation can be strong except in the strength of God, or safe except in His defense. The trust of our people in God should be declared on our national coins.

You will cause a device to be prepared without unnecessary delay with a motto expressing in the fewest and tersest words possible this national recognition.

It was found that the Act of Congress dated January 18, 1837, prescribed the mottoes and devices that should be placed upon the coins of the United States. This meant that the mint could make no changes without the enactment of additional legislation by the Congress. In December 1863, the Director of the Mint submitted designs for new one-cent coin, two-cent coin, and three-cent coin to Secretary Chase for approval. He proposed that upon the designs either OUR COUNTRY; OUR GOD or GOD, OUR TRUST should appear as a motto on the coins. In a letter to the Mint Director on December 9, 1863, Secretary Chase stated:

I approve your mottoes, only suggesting that on that with the Washington obverse the motto should begin with the word OUR, so as to read OUR GOD AND OUR COUNTRY. And on that with the shield, it should be changed so as to read: IN GOD WE TRUST.

The Congress passed Action April 22, 1864. This legislation changed the composition of the one-cent coin and authorized the minting of the two-cent coin. The Mint Director was directed to develop the designs for these coins for final approval of the Secretary. IN GOD WE TRUST first appeared on the 1864 two-cent coin.

The motto has been in continuous use on the one-cent coin since 1909, and on the ten-cent coin since 1916. It also has appeared on all gold coins and silver dollar coins, half-dollar coins, and quarter-dollar coins struck since July 1, 1908.

A law passed by the 84th Congress (P.L. 84-10) approved by the President on July 30, 1956, the President approved a Joint Resolution of the 84th Congress, declaring IN GOD WE TRUST the national motto of the United States. IN GOD WE TRUST was first used on paper money in 1957, when it appeared on the one-dollar silver certificate. The first paper currency bearing the motto entered circulation on October 1, 1957….

The above article is reprinted from www.ustreas.gov/ U.S. Treasury Dept.

Our National Floral Emblem

United States Code: Office of the Law Revision Council   Title 36, Patriotic Societies and Observances
Chapter 3, Section 187 National floral emblem
Executive Order: Proclamation No. 5574 THE ROSE PROCLAIMED THE NATIONAL FLORAL EMBLEM OF
THE UNITED STATES OF AMERICA

Proc. No. 5574, Nov. 20, 1986, 51 F. R. 42197, provided:

Americans have always loved the flowers with which God decorates our land. More often than any other flower, we hold the rose dear as the symbol of life and love and devotion, of beauty and eternity. For the love of man and woman, for the love of mankind and God, for the love of country, Americans who would speak the language of the heart do so with a rose.

We see proofs of this everywhere. The study of fossils reveals that the rose has existed in America for age upon age. We have always cultivated roses in our gardens. Our first President, George Washington, bred roses, and a variety he named after his mother is still grown today. The White House itself boasts a beautiful Rose Garden. We grow roses in all our fifty States. We find roses throughout our art, music, and literature. We decorate our celebrations and parades with roses. Most of all, we present roses to those we love, and we lavish them on our altars, our civil shrines, and the final resting places of our honored dead.

The American people have long held a special place in hearts for roses. Let us continue to cherish them, to honor the love and devotion they represent, and to bestow them on all we love just as God has bestowed them on us.

The Congress, by Senate Joint Resolution 159 (Pub. L. 99-449, now this section, has designated the rose as the National Floral Emblem of the United States and authorized and requested the President to issue a proclamation declaring this fact.

NOW, THEREFORE, I, RONALD REAGAN, President of the United States of America, do hereby proclaim the rose as the National Floral Emblem of the United States of America.

IN WITNESS WHEREOF, I have hereunto set my hand this twentieth day of November, in the year of our Lord nineteen hundred and eighty-six, and of the Independence of the United States of America the two hundred and eleventh.

Ronald Reagen

The Liberty Bell

A Symbol of American Freedom

The Liberty Bell, located within the Liberty Bell Pavilion on Market Street, Philadelphia

Each person reading the inscription of the Liberty Bell interprets the words to his own needs: *Proclaim LIBERTY throughout all the Land unto all the inhabitants thereof (Leviticus 25:10).* "In 1751, the Speaker of the Pennsylvania Assembly ordered a new bell for the State House. He asked that a Bible verse to [sic] be placed on the bell…. As the official bell of the Pennsylvania State House (today called Independence Hall) it rang many times for public announcements, but we remember times like July 8, 1776, when it rang to announce the first public reading of the Declaration of Independence." The first bell that arrived in Philadelphia cracked and was replaced by a second bell in 1753. "By 1846 a thin crack began to affect the sound of the [new] bell. The bell was repaired in 1846 and rang for a George Washington birthday celebration, but the bell cracked again and has not been rung since. No one knows why the bell cracked either time…. The bell weighs about 2000 pounds. It is made of 70% copper, 25% tin, and small amounts of lead, zinc, arsenic, gold, and silver. It hangs from what is believed to be its original yoke, made from American elm, also known as slippery elm." *(National Park Service: www.nps.gov) Photography by Courtesy of Independence National Historic Park*

Fort McHenry and the Star-Spangled Banner

The twenty-five hour battle between the British Navy and American forces began early in the morning of September 13, 1814, at Fort McHenry in Baltimore, Maryland. A young, 34-year-old attorney experienced the battle sounds from an eight-mile distance all through the night, having been detained by the British for his own protection during the battle. As dawn approached, and using a telescope to observe the Fort, he spyed the unfurled flag, 30 feet by 42 feet in size, raised victoriously over the Fort, the brilliant colors waving with such glory. So inspired by the scene, Key quickly wrote words that described what he saw and words that revealed his emotional verve into a poem, completing a total of four verses a few hours later. Key had copies of his poem printed and began disbursing them among his fellow patriots. The poem became known as "The Star-Spangled Banner." Emotions ran high about the second war for independence from England, known as the War of 1812. The words of the poem were set to the music of a well-known British drinking song, "To Anacreon in Heaven." The Library of Congress states: "…only in 1931, following a twenty-year effort during which more than forty bills and joint resolutions were introduced in Congress, was a law finally signed proclaiming "The Star Spangled Banner' to be the national anthem of the United States."

Oh, say can you see, by the dawn's early light,
What so proudly we hailed at the twilight's last gleaming?
Whose broad stripes and bright stars, through the perilous fight,
O'er the ramparts we watched, were so gallantly streaming?
And the rockets' red glare, the bomb bursting in air,
Gave proof through the night that our flag was still there.
O say, does that star-spangled banner yet wave
O'er the land of the free and the home of the brave?

On the shore, dimly seen through the mists of the deep,
Where the foe's haughty host in dread silence reposes,
What is that which the breeze, o'er the towering steep,
As it fitfully blows, now conceals, now discloses?
Now it catches the gleam of the morning's first beam,
In full glory reflected now shines on the stream:
"Tis the star-spangled banner! O long may it wave
O'er the land of the free and the home of the brave.

And where is that band who so vauntingly swore
That the havoc of war and the battle's confusion
A home and a country should leave us not more?
Their blood has wiped out their foul footstep's pollution.
No refuge could save the hireling and slave
From the terror of flight, or the gloom of the grave:
And the star-spangled banner in triumph doth wave
O'er the land of the free and the home of the brave.

Oh! thus be it ever, when freemen shall stand
Between their loved homes and the war's desolation!
Blest with victory and peace, may the heaven-rescued land
Praise the Power that hath made and preserved us a nation.
Then conquer we must, when our cause it is just,
And this be our motto: "In God is our trust."
And the star-spangled banner in triumph shall wave
O'er the land of the free and the home of the Brave!

In Our Nation's Capital

The United States Capitol

"The United States Capitol is among the most architecturally impressive and symbolically important buildings in the world. It has housed the meeting chambers of the Senate and the House of Representatives for almost two centuries. Begun in 1793, the Capitol has been built, burnt, rebuilt, extended, and restored: today, it stands as a monument not only to its builders but also to the American people and their government."*(www.aoc.gov)* It was the results of a competition for the best design that brought about America's most recognized structure. A Scottish physician, Dr. William Thornton, won the "$500 prize and a city lot" as a reward for his efforts, heeding the call suggested by then Secretary of State Thomas Jefferson in 1792. Grand marble terraces grace the west front of the Capitol, which were added to the building between 1884 and 1891. The East Front experienced structural changes that were completed in 1960 with an expansion of 32.5 feet, which added 102 rooms to the marble building. Continued restoration work has allowed the beauty of the building to be maintained at its grand design. *Photo by Marian Blank*

In Our Nation's Capital

The White House, Washington, D.C.

"For two hundred years, the White House has stood as a symbol of the Presidency, the United States government, and the American people. Its history, and the history of the nation's capital, began when President George Washington signed an Act of Congress in December of 1790 declaring that the federal government would reside in a district 'not exceeding ten miles square…on the river Potomac.' President Washington, together with city planner Pierre L'Enfant, chose the site for the new residence, which is now 1600 Pennsylvania Avenue. As preparations began for the new federal city, a competition was held to find a builder of the 'President's House.' Nine proposals were submitted, and Irish-born architect James Hoban won a gold medal for his practical and handsome design…. Construction began when the first cornerstone was laid in October 1792. Although President Washington oversaw the construction of the house, he never lived in it. It was not until 1800, when the White House was nearly completed that its first resident, President John Adams and his wife, Abigail, moved in…. [The White House] is the only private residence of a head of state that is open to the public, free of charge." *(www.whitehouse.gov)* *Photo by Shangle Photographics*

In Our Nation's Capital

The United States Supreme Court Building, Washington, D. C.

Words of value grace both the west entrance, with *Equal Justice Under the Law,* and the east entrance, with *Justice the Guardian of Liberty.* That style of guidance has been preserved since the first session of the court that took place on February 1, 1790, in New York City in the Royal Exchange Building. The Court has had many homes before settling into the new house in 1935. Philadelphia, Pennsylvania, provided chambers in Independence Hall and the City Hall from 1790 to 1800, at which time the Court moved to the new capital, Washington, D. C. When the Capitol was burned by the British in the War of 1812, the Court convened in a private residence. When the Capitol was restored for occupancy, the Supreme Court was lodged in what is referred to as the "Old Supreme Court Chamber" from 1816 to 1860, moving to the "Old Senate Chamber," where the Court maintained presence until this handsome marble structure was built. Sixteen marble columns support the heavily adorned portico and 100-foot wide oval plaza, delivering a strong character to a supreme building that is home to nine justices. *Photo by James Blank*

In Our Nation's Capital

The Washington Monument, Washington, D. C.

The Washington Monument Society, founded by John Marshall and James Madison in 1833, took up the cause to honor the outstanding patriot, George Washington, often referred to as the "Father of our Country." Many obstacles along the way slowed the completion of the monument, often to a stand still during the Civil War. The monument was finally dedicated February 21, 1885, and opened for public tours October 9, 1888. The building reaches 555 feet, 5 1/8th inches into the sky, with a thrusting "unadorned Egyptian obelisk" made of Maryland and Massachusetts marble, much granite and interior ironwork. A recent extensive restoration program has brought the building to a modern marvel, aided by private and corporate funds from patriot supporters. *Photo by James Blank*

In Our Nation's Capital

The Lincoln Memorial, Washington, D. C.

"The Lincoln Memorial stands at the west end of the National Mall as a neoclassical monument to the 16th President. The memorial, designed by Henry Bacon, after ancient Greek temples, stands 190 feet long, 119 feet wide, and almost 100 feet high. It is surrounded by a peristyle of thirty-six fluted Doric columns, one for each of the thirty-six states in the Union at the time of Lincoln's death, and two columns[sic] in antis at the entrance behind the colonnade…. Lying between the north and south chambers is the central hall containing the solitary figure of Lincoln sitting in contemplation…. Construction began in 1914, and the memorial was opened to the public in 1922." *(www.nps.gov)* The Memorial is not only a tribute to Abraham Lincoln but it is also a symbol of American Democracy and the freedom that has been maintained through the unity of the people of this nation. *Photo by James Blank*

In Our Nation's Capital

The Thomas Jefferson Memorial and the Tidal Basin, Washington, D.C.

"The Thomas Jefferson Memorial, modeled after the Pantheon of Rome, is America's foremost memorial to our third president. As an original adaptation of Neoclassical architecture, it is a key landmark in the monumental core of Washington, D. C. The circular, colonnaded structure in the classic style was introduced to this country by Thomas Jefferson. Architect John Russell Pope used Jefferson's own architectural tastes in the design of the Memorial. His intention was to synthesize Jefferson's contribution as a statesman, architect, President, drafter of the Declaration of Independence, advisor of the Constitution and founder of the University of Virginia…. The present-day location at the Tidal Basin was selected in 1937…. On November 15, 1939, a ceremony was held in which President Roosevelt laid the cornerstone of the Memorial" *(National Park Service)* The Memorial was officially dedicated on December 19, 1943, commemorating the 200th anniversary of Jefferson's birth. A nineteen-foot bronze statue of Thomas Jefferson, set upon a six-foot high, black-granite pedestal, graces the center of the rotunda, gazing out across the Tidal Basin toward the nation's capitol. "Each year the Jefferson Memorial plays host to various ceremonies, including annual Memorial exercises, Easter Sunrise Services and the ever-popular Cherry Blossom Festival. The Jefferson Memorial is administered and maintained by the National Park Service." *(National Park Service)* Photo by James Blank

Tomb of the Unknowns at Arlington National Cemetery, Arlington, Virginia

"The Tomb of the Unknowns, near the center of the cemetery, is one of Arlington's most popular tourist sites. The Tomb contains the remains of unknown American soldiers from World Wars I and II, the Korean Conflict and (until 1998) the Vietnam War. Each was presented with the Medal of Honor at the time of interment and the medals, as well as the flags which covered their caskets, are on display inside the Memorial Amphitheater, directly to the rear of the Tomb. The Tomb is guarded 24-hours-per-day and 365-days-per year by specially trained members of the 3rd United States Infantry (The Old Guard)." *(www.arlingtoncemetery.com)* The white Colorado-marble sarcophagus resides over the grave of the World War I unknown soldier; to the west are the marble crypts of the Unknown Soldiers of World War II, the Korean Conflict, and the crypt honoring the Vietnam Unknown, which now remains vacant since the Unknown, laid to rest in 1984, was tentatively identified and exhumed in 1998. *Photo by James Blank*

The Vietnam Veterans Memorial

"The Vietnam Veterans Memorial Wall contains the names of the 58,220 men and women who were killed and remain missing from that war. The names are etched on black granite panels that compose the Wall. The panels are arranged into two arms, extending from a central point to form a wide angle. Each arm points to either the Washington Monument or the Lincoln Memorial…bringing the Vietnam Memorial into an historical context on the National Mall. The Wall is built into the earth, below ground level. The area within the Wall's angle has been contoured to form a gentle sloped approach towards the center of the Wall…a place of quiet, calmness, and serenity." *(National Park Service) Photo by James Blank*

USS Arizona Memorial, Pearl Harbor, Honolulu, Hawaii, Island of Oahu

"The Memorial straddles the sunken hull of the battleship USS Arizona and commemorates the December 7, 1941, Japanese attack on Pearl Harbor. The Memorial was dedicated in 1962, and became a National Park Service area in 1980." *(www.nps.gov)* "The 7 December 1941 Japanese raid on Pearl Harbor was one of the great defining moments in history. A single carefully-planned and well-executed stroke removed the United States Navy's battleship force as a possible threat to the Japanese Empire's southward expansion." *(U.S. Dept. of the Navy)* The United States Congress declared war on the nation of Japan on December 8, 1941, and accepted a decisive surrender on August 15, 1945. *Photo by James Blank*

The United States Marine Corps War Memorial, Arlington, Virginia

"The Marine Corps War Memorial stands as a symbol of this grateful Nation's esteem for the honored dead of the U. S. Marine Corps. While the statue depicts one of the most famous incidents of World War II, the memorial is dedicated to all Marines who have given their lives in the defense of the United States since 1775…. Burnished in gold on the granite [base] are the names and dates of every principal Marine Corps engagement since the founding of the Corps, as well as the inscription: 'In honor and in memory of the men of the United States Marine Corps who have given their lives to their country since November 10, 1775.' Also inscribed on the base is the tribute of Fleet Adm. Chester W. Nimitz to the fighting men on Iwo Jima: 'Uncommon Valor was a Common Virtue.' *(www.nps.gov)* The flag flies twenty-four hours a day at the end of a sixty-foot bronze pole. *Photo by James Blank*

The Continental Army at Valley Forge

At Valley Forge National Historical Park, Valley Forge, Pennsylvania

Valley Forge is one of the best-known sites of the American Revolution. The National Park Service states that "On December 19, 1777, when Washington's army marched into camp at Valley Forge, tired, cold, and ill-equipped, it was lacking in much of the training essential for consistent success on the battlefield. On June 19, 1778, after a six-month encampment, this same army emerged to pursue and successfully engaged Lt. Gen. Sir Henry Clinton's British army at the Battle of Monmouth in New Jersey. The ordered ranks, martial appearance, revived spirit, and fighting skill of the American soldiers spoke of a great transformation having occurred amidst the cold, sickness, and hardship that was Valley Forge.

"[One of the men] most responsible for this transformation was Friedrich Wilhelm von Steuben, onetime member of the elite General Staff of Frederick the Great, king of Prussia. No longer in the Prussian army, indeed without employment of any kind, von Steuben offered his military skills to the patriot cause. When he arrived at Valley Forge from France on February 23, 1778, he was armed with a letter of introduction from Benjamin Franklin. Washington saw great promise in the Prussian and almost immediately assigned him the duties of Acting Inspector General with the task of developing and carrying out an effective training program."

Typical of the barracks for the soldier of the Continental Army, small huts were quickly constructed after arriving on December 19, 1777. The huts offered protection from miserably cold and snowy weather during the winter months of their occupation at Valley Forge. The soldiers suffered and existed on substandard rations, when they were available. "About 800 soldiers served in each of the sixteen brigades at Valley Forge. An estimated 34,577 pounds of meat and 168 barrels of flour per day were needed to feed the army. Soldiers relied on their home states or the Continental Congress to supply food, clothing and equipment. Shortages varied widely between the regiments. Any number of misfortunes—spoilage, bad roads, or capture by British foragers—could prevent supplies from reaching camp. General [Anthony] Wayne used troops and went to New Jersey to commandeer food when shortages occured. Owners concealed their animals in the pine woods. He was so successful at obtaining supplies that he became known as the Drover." *(National Park Service) Photo by James Blank*

The Gettysburg Address

The Soldiers Memorial in the National Cemetery, Gettysburg National Military Park, Gettysburg, Pennsylvania

It was at this site on November 19, 1863 that President Abraham Lincoln delivered his famous Gettysburg Address:

Fourscore and seven years ago our fathers brought forth on this continent a new nation, conceived in liberty and dedicated to the proposition that all men are created equal. Now we are engaged in a great civil war testing whether that nation, or any nation so conceived and so dedicated, can long endure. We are met on a great battlefield of that war. We have come to dedicate a portion of that field as a final resting-place for those who here gave their lives that that nation might live. It is altogether fitting and proper that we should do this. But, in a larger sense, we cannot dedicate—we cannot consecrate—we cannot hallow—this ground. The brave men, living and dead, who struggled here have consecrated it far above our poor power to add or detract. The world will little note, nor long remember what we say here, but it can never forget what they did here. It is for us the living, rather, to be dedicated here to the unfinished work which they who fought here have thus far so nobly advanced. It is rather for us to be here dedicated to the great task remaining before us—that from these honored dead we take increased devotion to that cause for which they gave the last full measure of devotion—that we here highly resolve that these dead shall not have died in vain— that this nation, under God, shall have a new birth of freedom—and that government of the people, by the people, for the people, shall not perish from the earth.

Photo by James Blank

The Minuteman

The Minuteman Statue, Lexington, Massachusetts

Placed on the Lexington Green in 1900, this bronze statue of the Minuteman represents Captain John Parker, leader of the militia who exchanged fire with British troops on April 19, 1775. The statue commemorates the colonial militiamen who were *on-the-ready* to defend the right of the American colonies to resist England's economic policies. Having been notified by Paul Revere that the British troops were going to Concord to seize the patriot arms supply, the well-trained militia and minute men were ready for their advance. Shots were fired on the Lexington Common where the war for independence from England began. Who fired the first shot is unknown, but several militia men were killed. Behind the statue is a boulder inscribed with Parker's words: "Stand your ground; don't fire unless fired upon, but if they mean to have a war, let it begin here." *Photo by Robert D. Shangle*

The Betsy Ross House, 239 Arch Street, Philadelphia

Elizabeth (Betsy) Griscom and John Ross opened their upholstery shop in this rented house on Arch Street in 1775. The two-and-one-half story Georgian-style house was built around 1740. Betsy, whose husband was killed in 1776 while guarding ammunition, was secretly commissioned by the Continental Congress in May, 1776, to sew the first flag of the new nation, which she completed in June. The following year "on June 14, 1777, the Continental Congress, seeking to promote national pride and unity, adopted the national flag. 'Resolved: that the flag of the United States be thirteen stripes, alternate red and white; that the union be thirteen stars, white in a blue field, representing a new constellation'." There has been some controversy for many years as to the authenticity of the story of the Betsy Ross flag. However, a claim brought forth in 1870 was made public by her grandson, William J. Canby:

> *It is not tradition, it is report from the lips of the principal participator in the transact, directly told not to one or two, but a dozen or more living witnesses, of which I myself am one, though but a little boy when I heard it…Colonel Ross with Robert Morris and General Washington, called on Mrs. Ross and told her they were a committee of Congress, and wanted her to make a flag from the drawing, a rough one, which, upon her suggestions, was redrawn by General Washington in pencil in her back parlor. This was prior to the Declaration of Independence. I fix the date to be during Washington's visit to Congress from New York in June, 1776 when he came to confer upon the affairs of the Army, the flag being no doubt, one of these affairs."*

Photo by James Blank

Fort Ticonderoga, Ticonderoga, New York

North of the city of Albany, New York, is old Fort Ticonderoga, a place steeped in history that goes back to 1755. The French built the Fort and named it Fort Carillon. It was in a strategic location, between Lake George and Lake Champlain, controlling the route between the Hudson River Valley and Canada. The French were making inroads for their dominance in the area. In July 1758 the first Battle of Ticonderoga took place during the French and Indian War, the French winning the battle. Within a year's time England's General Jeffery Amhurst captured the fort, renaming it Fort Ticonderoga. Seventeen years later the war for Independence between the Americans and the English began at Lexington, Massachusetts. In less than a month, Ethan Allen and his Green Mountain Boys stormed the fort and took control in another Battle of Ticonderoga. In 1777 the British forced the Patriot forces out of the fort and took possession. To solve its occupation, the British abandoned the fort and burned the buildings. It was in 1909 that Fort Ticonderoga was restored and turned into a museum. *Photo by James Blank*

A replica of the North Bridge at Concord, Massachusetts

On April 19, 1775, British troops arrived and engaged in their second conflict of the day with Patriot forces, loosely organized but determined to restrict the British from obtaining the stored arms and ammunition they held in Concord. The Patriots had been informed of British troop movement by Paul Revere and William Dawes, who rode through the night notifying their countrymen of the impending invasion. The bridge was first built in 1750 on land donated by Jonathan Buttrick. Loose oak planking, which created the bridge surface, was removed by the British to impede the Patriots. *Photo by Robert D. Shangle*

Bunker Hill Monument, Boston National Historic Park, Charlestown, Massachusetts

Bunker Hill and Breeds' Hill are the sites of the first major battle of the American Revolution occurring on June 17, 1775, led by Col. William Prescott of Massachusetts. About 1,500 Patriot soldiers were present, made up of men from Massachusetts, New Hampshire, led by John Stark, and Connecticut, led by Israel Putnam. The American soldiers were forced to retreat since they had used all their ammunition, however, their fighting tactics were demoralizing to the British and uplifting to the troops. Courage and hope for independence came to the fearful colonists. *Photo by Robert D. Shangle*

Mount Vernon, Mt. Vernon, Virginia

Masterfully preserved and restored with many original items, Mount Vernon, home to George and Martha Washington, the nation's first President and First Lady, resides on acreage that reveals the early history of American gentry life. The house was originally built in 1735. George inherited the house and about 2,000 acres of land in 1761, where he and his wife lived before, during, and after the Revolutionary War. Both are buried in family tombs on the grounds. The house and grounds remained with the Washington family until 1858. *Photo by James Blank*

Monticello, home to President Thomas Jefferson, Third President of the United States, Charlottesville, Virginia

Designed and built by Thomas Jefferson, this forty-three room, architectural masterpiece encompasses about 11,000-square-feet of living area. Its overall length is 110 feet and its width is 87 feet 9 inches. Eight fireplaces and two wood-burning stoves were used to heat the house. Candles and oil lamps provided illumination. Construction began in 1769 and after several remodeling efforts was completed in 1809. Perhaps the most recognized house in America, the East Front of the house is displayed on the U. S. nickel coin, while the West Front is displayed here. *Photo by Shangle Photographics*

The United States Miliary Academy, West Point, New York

West Point is the oldest continuously occupied military post in America. President Thomas Jefferson signed legislation establishing the United States Military Academy at West Point in 1802. Distinguished graduates include Robert E. Lee, Ulysses Grant, Douglas MacArthur, Dwight D. Eisenhower, Omar Bradley, George Patton, and Mark Clark. Douglas MacArthur was superintendent of the Academy following World War I. *Photo by Robert D. Shangle*

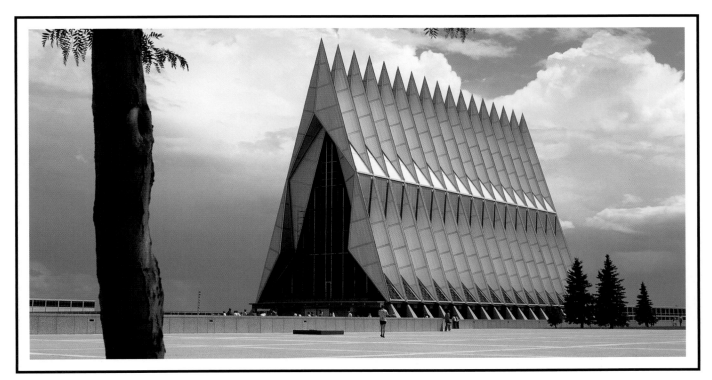

The Cadet Chapel, United States Air Force Academy, Colorado Springs, Colorado

It was April 1, 1954, when Dwight D. Eisenhower, 34th President of the United States, authorized the creation of the United States Air Force Academy, following several years of extensive study by a select committee. Though academic activity began in July, 1955, at nearby Lowery Air Force Base in Denver, the facilities were not officially occupied until August, 1958. The architecturally acclaimed Cadet Chapel completed in 1963 provides a religious center for many faiths, with programs dedicated to devotional awareness. *Photo by James Blank*

The United State Naval Academy, Annapolis, Maryland

The United States Navy was born during the American Revolution when the need for a naval force to match the British Navy became apparent. Later in 1845 George Bancroft, Secretary of the Navy under President Polk, initiated the establishment of the United States Naval Academy at Annapolis, Maryland. The original site was a ten-acre Army Post named Fort Stevens. Today, the Academy is made up of over 338 acres. The original student body of fifty young men has now grown to a brigade over 4,000 young men and women. *Photo by Robert D. Shangle*

The United States Coast Guard Academy, New London, Connecticut

The academy was founded in 1876 with nine cadets, beginning their training aboard the schooner *Dobbin*. Today's academy was born with the 1915 merger of the Life Saving Service and Revenue Cutter Service. The academy was moved to its present location in New London in 1932. Approximately 275 young men and women enter the academy each July. *Photo by Robert D. Shangle*

Still Creek, Mt. Hood National Forest in the Cascade Mountains in Oregon An example of nature's beauty found in many places in the United States of America. *Photo by Shangle Photographics*

The Beauty of America

We Americans love to do a little occasional self-puffery, preening ourselves on what we have done as a country and expect to do in the future. A sense of optimism pervades our national consciousness and penetrates the manifold activities that we engage in on a daily basis. Our positive attitudes and expansive nature are inspired in some measure by the bountiful land which sustains us. In these days when the natural arrangement of the world seems to be in some jeopardy from growing populations and human activities, we have turned more of our attention to the care and preservation of our marvelous corner of it.

Both our material progress as a nation and our optimistic outlook have been fueled by the wealth of our lands and waters. Being a practical people, we are beginning to see the wisdom of responsible use of our resources. But beyond the practicality is an emotional attachment to the land that draws upon a long tradition. Many generations have dwelt in the land now called the United States. Their consciousness and character have always been changed in some degree by the region they call home. Even today's mobile Americans are usually identifiable by the part of the country from where they hail. The New Englander, tough and resourceful, is following in the tradition of his forbearer, who had to be both innovative and hardworking to gain a livelihood from their land-sea environment. The Plainsman, under an endless vault of sky reaching to a horizon that is a remote mystery, puts more of his faith in the Divinity than in the works of man, whose scale is dwarfed by his natural setting and whose fate seems wholly captive to the whims of weather. The people of the Plains cluster in

Bellingrath Garden and Home South of Mobile at Theodore is an art form alive with ever-changing color., the 65-acre Bellingrath Garden that surrounds the house that now is a memory museum to Walter and Bessie Morse Bellingrath. As the seasons change so do the available blooming plants, creating a kaleidoscope of freshness and aroma year around. Delicate in appearance but strong and vigorous, the Camellia provides an array of color during the winter months, supported by daffodils, azaleas and other flowering bushes, flowering trees, rose gardens, and other floral varieties. *Photo by Shangle Photographics*

small towns and medium-sized cities; they are friendly and open, putting great value on personal relationships, and rarely concentrate in such large numbers that these relationships are lost.

The limitless open reaches of the Southwest seem to nurture another kind of individuality. The Texan is not awed by the vastness of his surroundings, possibly because he is less dependent on what grows on them than is the Plainsman to the north. Because much of his wealth comes from beneath the surface, he can confront the more unruly moods of nature with confidence. His glittering cities seem to be an expression of his assurance that everything is possible.

Those who find their home in the highlands are likely to be of a still different stripe. The Appalachians have their hill people, from north Georgia through Tennessee, the Carolinas, Virginia and on up the eastern states, who hold the world more at arm's length than do the people of the Piedmont and Plains areas. And the one who establishes his sanctuary on the slopes of the Rocky or Cascade mountains is just as likely to put a high value on the relative scarcity of other folks in his neighborhood.

The lavish variety of landscapes and weather regimes that occur throughout the land has been a strong magnet to settlement. With the enrollment of Alaska and Hawaii on the roster of states, this diversity has become even more emphatic. The nation now reaches north into the Arctic and south into the Tropics. The riches of the earth are expressed in so many different ways in the United States that when a person stops to consider the abundance and variety of it all, he is at a terrible disadvantage. The bounty of natural forms has outstripped the ability of human language to describe it. Some of the more eloquent among us have immortalized parts of it in novels, plays, and poems, never able to encapsulate the grandeur of the country in a work of literature.

There is a kind of majestic orchestration to the primary continental features. The wide interior valley of the Mississippi River reaches from nearly the Canadian border to the Gulf of Mexico, extending far to the east and west of the storied river that rules like a watery divinity over its fate. The big river's countless tributaries, big and little, drain this fertile midsection. For a long time much of this rich basin was considered a waste, a desert, but once its fertility was demonstrated and its abundant water resources tapped, it quickly outstripped every other river valley on earth in the production of foodstuffs. On the west and east, the north-south trending Rocky and Appalachian mountains stretch out along the valley's flanks. Their heights nourish the rivers that flow to the Mississippi and help moderate the weather of the valley.

Southwest of the Rockies in the high plateau country, the many rivers manifest in a dramatic way their ability to shape the land. With powerful down-cutting currents, they have fashioned giant clefts in the earth over many millions of years, endlessly flowing through these spectacular canyons of their own creation. The Pacific Ocean side itself is a study in a variety of beauty, from the deserts of southern California to the mountain-and-water environments of the Northwest. The mountains come in many shapes and sizes. There are, for example, the monolithic Sierras, considered by some as being unequalled in majestic mountain scenery. But that claim is also made for the separate, symmetrical volcanic peaks of the Cascades. Alaska and Hawaii add more extravagance: Alaska has the continent's biggest mountains and ice fields, and Hawaii boasts of the tropical waters on shores that once flowed as lava.

This collection of scenes from all fifty states in the Union provides an admirable sample of the immense and ever changing tableau that is the United States.

Alaska: 49th State: January 3, 1959—Capital: Juneau   State Motto: *North to the Future*
State Bird: Willow Ptarmigan   State Flower: Forget-Me-Not   State Song: "Alaska's Flag"   State Tree: Sitka Spruce

Portage Lake at Portage Glacier Recreation Area, east of Anchorage Icebergs, massive chunks of ice that have detached from Portage Glacier, float in the lake created by the glacier. Within itself Alaska is the biggest of the fifty states in the Union but the smallest in population. There are huge mountains, such as Mt. McKinley, 20,320 feet, at Denali National Park & Preserve, the highest mountain in the United States, and many more majestic mountains. There are countless ice fields and glaciers, and rivers, streams and lakes that beckon visitors. Wildlife is abundant: grizzly bear and brown bear, wolves, Dall sheep and moose, caribou, polar bear, musk ox, and Gray wolf. Fishing is outstanding, both sport and commercial, which is a leading economic industry. Natural resources such as oil and natural gas are abundant. Yet there is very little farming as is common in the United States. Days are long in the summer, with a short growing season. Days are short in the winter. *Photo by Robert D. Shangle*

Our Valley of Plenty

There is an enormous piece of real estate lying between the Rocky and Appalachian mountains, running from Canada to the Gulf of Mexico, that is considered by many as the Valley of Plenty. Food is what is produced here, and lots of it. As you look across the biggest cornfields found anywhere in the world, where you are unable to see across to the other side of the field, an Iowa farmer might be heard to say, "Now you know where all the food comes from." Food is the thing, from the wheatfields of the Dakotas and the cornfields of Iowa down to the rice paddies and kingdom-sized cattle ranches along the Texas Gulf Coast. The story of the Mississippi River watershed is one of cultivation.

The serene beauty of a well-tended field is no better exemplified than on these fertile plains and rolling hills where nature's original ingredients are combined by man to grow his food. Man's intervention has created a kind of beauty that nature, left to herself, has not been able to achieve in such a landscape. The purely natural look comes into its own in spectacle—mighty rivers, steep canyons, stormy oceans, hulking mountains, and the like. But on a wide valley, plateau, or plain, human-scale arrangements add interest to a landscape that is otherwise formless. A textured field, whether in the tender new growth of springtime, in full summer glory, or stripped bare after the harvest, is a thing of beauty; as moving in its fullness as a snow-capped glaciated spire is for entirely different reasons.

Arizona: 48th State: February 14, 1912—State Capital: Phoenix State Motto: *God Enriches*
State Bird: Cactus Wren   State Flower: Saguaro Cactus Blossom   State Song: "Arizona"   State Tree: Palo Verde

The Grand Canyon "No other place on earth looks quite like it" is what the Grand Canyon National Park states about the vast hypnotic presence of the Grand Canyon, located entirely in northern Arizona. Hot in the summer and cold in the winter. The north rim in the distance can be visited between the months of May and October, but is closed due to heavy snow during the remaining months. Numerous hiking trails purvey access for investigation of the nine separate rock layers that can be seen. The degree of difficulty of the hiking trails is remarkable and caution is expressed for the would-be hiker. From the south rim, which is accessible year-round, to the north rim, the width varies from 10 to 18 miles. The canyon depth varies from about 5,000 feet to 6,000 feet, from the rim to the carving Colorado River below, having forced its way through the rock layers revealing the oldest aged rock at the bottom of the canyon, recorded to be from half-a-billion to a billion-years old. Spanish explorer Francisco Vásquez de Coronado was the first European to view the canyon in 1540. In 1850 the U. S. Army explored the canyon land and in 1869 American geologist John Wesley Powell and his entourage completed the daring navigation through the canyon. *Photography by Shangle Photographics*

Arkansas: 25th State: June 15, 1836—Capital: Little Rock   State Motto: *The People Rule*
State Bird: Mockingbird   State Flower: Apple Blossom   State Song: "Arkansas"   State Tree: Pine

Beaver Lake, Northwest Arkansas   This 28,000-acre lake is just one of the several spawling lake sites in Arkansas. Beaver Lake provides rugged terrain contrasted by the scenic natural beauty of the Ozark Mountains, famed for its pristine beauty and recreation opportunities. Arkansas was first explored by Hernando de Soto in 1541, but France took possession of the area with its first settler in 1686. Following its acquisition by the United States in 1803 as part of the Louisiana Purchase, the Arkansas Territory was established in 1819 and development began. Just a few miles south of Beaver Lake is the city of Fayetteville, home to the University of Arkansas established in 1871, opening its doors to students in 1872. There are six national parks and forty state parks within the state's boundary. *Photo by James Blank*

So agriculture, sometimes, and in some places, is on the side of the angels, environmentally speaking. Man's interference with nature produces blessings instead of calamities. Perhaps "interference" is not the word. "Cooperation" may be more precise, when farming is the issue—especially in the Midwest. The relationship is synergistic, producing out of man-and-nature's contributions something greater, materially and esthetically, than the sum of the separate elements. A bountiful crop of pure beauty is in the relationship itself: we have not made a better bargain with the earth than when we plant it. Farming is, to be sure, the first impulse of a civilized society. "Where tillage begins," Daniel Webster said, "other arts follow."

That part of the Midwest that lies on the western slope of the Mississippi Basin is called the Plains. The valley of the other side of the big river is also the Midwest, but with a difference. The eastern part is more heavily populated, hillier, and even mountainous where the Appalachian slopes reach into them. But despite some very large cities in Ohio, Indiana, and Illinois, it still has an essentially rural, open look, with big pastures and grain fields that spread in a checkerboard pattern across a flat or gently rolling land. Its vistas usually betray the hand of man, and textures of his fields dominate the horizon rather than disappear into it.

The Plains—the *real* Plains—are another world, different from any other kind of landscape within the United States. They include Iowa, Kansas, Nebraska, North Dakota, South Dakota, and parts of Montana, Wyoming, Colorado, Minnesota and Missouri. What are the Plains? They are vast, empty spaces to begin with. They may be flat or they may be gently undulating, but their overwhelming impact is of space. Even those individuals who live there all their lives, who know no other place in the world, sometimes feel frightened by the sense of weight that those limitless horizons impose. Someone standing alone under a sky that has no beginning

California: 31st State: September 9, 1850—Sacramento   State Motto: *Eureka!*

State Bird: California Valley Quail   State Flower: Golden Poppy   State Song: "I Love You, California"   State Tree: California Redwood

Mount Lassen and Manzanita Lake, Lassen National Volcanic Park, Northern California Mount Lassen is the centerpiece of a ridge of cinder cones in Lassen Volcanic National Park, which actually erupted through 1914 to 1917, throwing rocks and spewing hot lava over the surrounding valley. Some of the cones in this area are very young, having been born within the past 500 years. The heart of the Lassen country is open only by trail, but the entire park is within a day's hiking distance of a road. The high road opens up an extraordinary vista reaching far beyond the confines of the park: Mount Shasta on the northwest, the Sierra Mountains to the south, and the jumble of mountains on the west. Northern California is far removed from southern California in appearance: rugged mountainous terrain, heavily clothed in evergreen trees, moving south into central California that leads to the agricultural center of the state, possessed of more flat, rich producing soil. The rugged Sierras pierce south along the eastern side while the dry western portion of the state leads to the remarkable California Pacific shore. The famous California Missions are spread from north of San Francisco in western California down to San Diego, near the southern United States boundary leading to Mexico. *Photo by James Blank*

and no end may begin to feel like a fish at the bottom of the sea, if he stays there very long. Watching the sun go down on the prairie, the only feature that doesn't go melting off over the far horizon is oneself. Standing there, shorn of pretensions, is an experience that puts new contours into the grooves of memory. The individual consciousness, before the sweep of the boundless prairie, abandons any such arrogant ambition as mastering this land. You don't subdue something that is so beyond your conceptual frame. You submit to it, rather. You accept whatever it is going to let you have.

That is why Plains dwellers, generally, are fatalists. But cheerful fatalists. They seem to value personal relationships more than those whose horizons are more readily definable. Their world is mostly flat and pretty much featureless. As far as they can see, everything is more-or-less horizontal, up to a sharply etched horizon that seems to drop off into mystery. Nature is a crushing presence.

The sun is really the leading actor in the Plains drama. Its light is spread out over an unending canvas that gives it back in a radiance submerging all differences. A marine metaphor seems to fit the Plains. They are a sea, a sea where your own fortunes are of no consequence, like the chaff that is swept in scudding whorls across the dry earth when a storm approaches.

And the Plains dweller knows about storms. Violent manifestations from the heavens are expected at some seasons of the year. Weather is both the beauty and the bane of the Midwesterner, the Plainsman, the farmer. The open land offers no protection from the weather in its merciless and savage moods. The storm that brings welcomed rain after a long dry spell may exact a payment in the form of a funnel cloud whose terrifying winds destroy everything in its path. Freezing cold and stifling heat visit the Midwest in their turn, but between these extremes, a soft breeze can bring exhilaration to the spirit or soothe away the accumulated heat of a long working day in the fields.

The mystery of the far-reaching Plains has never really been solved. The building of the Rocky Mountains may have had much to do with the original conformation of the land that sloped away from the mountains to the ancestral Mississippi. Streams from that Continental Divide spread deep alluvial layers over the land during millions of years. And the glaciers in their periodic visits brought down topsoil that built the wide valley into one of the world's most fertile regions.

Midwesterners have a special feeling for their homeland. Someone who has been there a long time, who is the third, fourth, or fifth generation of his family in the same place, is likely to believe in his very being that there is no place else to live in the world. The emptiness that brings the sky close to the ground holds no terror for someone who has been partners with it for a lifetime. The spaciousness is friendly spaciousness to someone who knows that both joy and woe are the lot of those who are subject to its whims. He accepts it, submits to it, whatever there is in store, and that way he gains an abiding certainty that he belongs to it, more than he could to any other part of the world. The limitless Plains have romance for him. Mountain walls around the perimeter of his sky would give him claustrophobia.

The Tributaries

The "featureless" Plains do have reference points, after all: the great rivers that reach into the interior

Colorado: 38th State: August 1, 1876—Capital: Denver   State Motto: *Nothing without Providence*

State Bird: Lark Bunting   State Flower: Rocky Mountain Columbine   State Song: "Where the Columbines Grow"   State Tree: Colorado Blue Spruce

Maroon Bells-Snowmass Wilderness   The twin peaks of the Maroon Bells push their way to a height of 14,146 feet above sea level. Below the peaks is Maroon Lake, cradled in a U-shaped alpine valley that takes command of the premises. Several companion peaks soar to heights over 14,000 feet, and many more exceed 9,000 feet. National Forest lands include the Gunnison and White rivers, both perfect for the recreation seeker: skiing and snowmobiling are great winter activities; hiking, photography, fishing, horseback riding, camping, boating and white water rafting are just a few suggestions. The Rocky Mountains dominate the western two-thirds of the state while the wide-open Great Plains spread eastward from the mountains. The land known as Colorado was first occupied by various Native American tribes: the Arapahoe, Utes, and the Anasazi, the ancestral tribe of today's Pueblo people. Spain arrived first to the area, losing control to the French who sold the land by way of the Louisiana Purchase in 1803. Mexico lost their Colorado land following the Mexican War of 1846-48. Mining has been a major economical foundation to the state, drawing miners and settlers to the state after the 1850s. *Photo by James Blank*

Connecticut: 5th State: January 9, 1788—Capital: Hartford   State Motto: *He who transplanted still sustains.*
State Bird: American Robin   State Flower: Mountain Laurel   State Song: "Yankee Doodle"   State Tree: White Oak

At Mystic, along the Mystic River   The seaport village of Mystic has maintained its maritime importance since its settlement in the 1600s. Mystic River has been home to several shipbuilding businesses that built and launched hundreds of ships out to the sea. The Intercoastal Waterway of Long Island Sound fronts most of the jagged shoreline of Connecticut, where the waters of the Atlantic Ocean have influenced the Connecticut economy. Whaling and fishing once were of great importance to the citizens of the state. Dutch explorer Adriaen Block claimed the area in 1614, sailing the coastline and up the Connecticut River. The English, who arrived in 1633, soon developed firm towns, which in 1636 were joined together to form the Colony of Connecticut. In 1665 the colonies of Connecticut and New Haven, which was founded in 1638, united. The U. S. Coast Guard Academy is located in New London, taking root in 1876 and establishing its home on the Thames River in 1932. *Photo by Shangle Photographics*

of the wide basin. The longest, wildest, and probably the most unpredictable of these lifelines is the Missouri River. More than any other river except the Mississippi itself, the Missouri is both the doing and the undoing of millions of square miles of plains. It and its tributaries, such as Nebraska's Platte, are the throbbing nervous system of most of the basin states west of the Mississippi. As befits a river of the Plains, the Missouri starts wandering all over its bed as soon as it gets past the clearly defined banks of its headwaters in Montana. The river is still regarded by those who live in its domain as godlike in power, capable of wreaking death and destruction in its demonic moods. Combining with a big tributary like the Republican or Kansas rivers, it has come up with some of the biggest and most costly floods in this country's history. Like the Mississippi, the Missouri was an avenue of steamboat traffic when those romantic carriers were in their heyday. And like the bigger stream, it swallowed up a good many of the boats when they got hung up on a sandbar or other unforeseeable underwater hazard. They had to cope, too, with a shifting channel that often decided to go somewhere else. One of the tongue-in-cheek recipes of that era for a proper "Big Muddy" steamboat required that it draw very little water; that it have lots of sternwheel muscle; that it be hinged in the middle; that it be able to suck up a sandbar if it couldn't climb over it (and on those occasions when the river escaped from under it); and it have the resources to climb a bank and travel across a cornfield to wherever the river had decided to relocate.

Bigger even than the Missouri in terms of water volume, the other main tributary of the Mississippi—the Ohio River—rules the eastern slopes of the mid-continental basin. Much of the Ohio River Valley is mountainous, or at least hilly, carrying the westward-reaching foothills of the Appalachians in eastern Ohio, West Virginia, southern Indiana, and Kentucky. The river has flooded often. In times of heavy rain or snow, its seventy-five tributaries pour a fearsome torrent into the broad waterway. When the volume exceeds the carrying capacity of the river—about once a generation—a flood spreads over the valley, inundating communities along the Ohio's banks. Pittsburgh, Cincinnati, Louisville, Cairo, and other communities have been washed by its waters in the past. Some of the Ohio's super floods have filled the valley from hill to hill, according to Indian legends. The flooding river, more than any other stream, has been responsible for the Mississippi's memorable rampages, pouring five times as much water into the lower Mississippi as the combined flow of the Missouri and the upper Mississippi.

Western Pennsylvania's Monongahela and Allegheny rivers come together at Pittsburgh to create the Ohio River. The big waterway, coursing through its softly rolling valley, has been compared to German's Rhone River, from two perspectives: its photogenic valley and its busy barge traffic. The beautiful Ohio is one of the world's most heavily used rivers. Its banks are lined with forests and factories, the natural features providing landmarks for river pilots by day, the man-made ones gleaming from the bank sides at night.

The Mississippi River

The Mississippi is the Father of Waters. Its length, nearly 2,400 miles, and the volume of water it carries, places it in the "big daddy" class. A few rivers of the world, like the Congo and the Amazon, are bigger, or drain even more territory. But none of these other areas can match the Mississippi basin for productivity. The river and its tributaries control the destiny of the vast Midwest and Plains. A map of the valley's river system

Delaware: 1st State: December 7, 1787—Capital: Dover State Motto: *Liberty and Independence*

State Bird: Blue Hen Chicken   State Flower: Peach Blossom   State Song: "Our Delaware"   State Tree: American Holly

Legislative Hall, Dover This Georgian Revival brick structure was built in 1933 and is home to Delaware's legislature. The Senate and House Chambers are located within the 18th-century styled building, as well as housing the Governor's ceremonial office. Delaware has the distinction of being the first of the original thirteen colonies to ratify the United States Constitution. The first settlers to the land were the Dutch in 1631, settling near the present-day town of Lewes, recognized as the first town in Delaware. The Dutch presence was short lived and the Swedes arrived in 1638, settling in present-day Wilmington. Not to be outdone, the Dutch reappeared, ousting the Swedes in 1655. The British campaign in 1664 rousted the settlements from the Dutch, claiming possession. *Photo by Shangle Photographicss*

53

looks something like an anatomical study of the body's veins and arteries. Each of the five primary tributaries is mightier than most of the country's other rivers. The Missouri, born far over in southwest Montana, is even longer than the parent stream—2,700 miles in length. The Ohio River, coming into its big valley on the eastern slope, almost doubles the flow of the Mississippi when the two join north of St. Louis Missouri. Three other navigable tributaries—the Illinois, Arkansas, and Ouachita—help bring river shipping into the well-watered interior.

Except when the very biggest floods come on the Mississippi system, the engineering and technology of today have taken much of the uncertainty out of river transportation. It is a far cry from the river of the steamboat pilots, those godlike beings sketched in the admiring detail by Mark Twain's *Life on the Mississippi*. The skillful pilots guided their unwieldy charges through shifting channels, treacherous shoals, and submerged debris on the long run from St. Paul to New Orleans.

The Mississippi begins a hundred miles or so from the Canadian border at two-pronged Lake Itasca, one of Minnesota's 15,000-plus big and little-pond like lakes. The headwaters are not much more than the flow that would come from an open fire hydrant. Summer tourists at the lake do the obligatory "walk across the Mississippi" where the rivulet leaves the lake, either wading or stepping over the twenty-foot width on a bridge of rocks. The only boats that can negotiate this stretch of the Mississippi are canoes. The little river is practically invisible as it wanders through the marshy wilds of northern Minnesota for the forty miles to Bemidji, then turns east and south to begin that long, majestic swing through the heart of the continent and on to the Gulf of Mexico.

The Mississippi is America's trademark. It is the physical feature that identifies this country more truly than any other, being entirely an American river. In its crooked north-south journey, the river becomes many

Florida: 27th State: March 3, 1845—Capital: Tallahassee State Motto: *In God We Trust*
State Bird: Mockingbird   State Flower: Orange Blossom   State Song: "Suwanee River"   State Tree: Sabel Palm

The Castillo de San Marcos National Monument at St. Augustine Built along the shore of Matanza Bay, the Castillo was constructed between 1672 and 1695. The Castillo was built by the Spanish to guard St. Augustine against the invasions by the English who had settlements north in Georgia and the Carolinas. England laid claim to the area from 1763 to 1783, returning it to Spain under the Treaty of Paris. Spain sold Florida to the United States in 1821. The Castillo was renamed Fort Marion and became a National Monument in 1924 and became part of the National Park system in 1933. The original name was restored in 1942. Throughout its career, the Castillo never fell into enemy hands during any conflict. It is believed that Spanish Explorer Don Juan Ponce de Leon first sighted the land he named *La Florida* on March 27, 1513. Don Pedro Menendez de Aviles, the new governor, arrived to the area on the Feast Day of St. Augustine, August 28, 1565, and shortly thereafter took over the site of the Timucuan Indian village that Aviles named St. Augustine. Known as the oldest permanent European settlement on the North American continent, St. Augustine was established fifty-five years before the landing of the Pilgrims in Massachusetts in 1620. *Photo by Shangle Photographics*

Stone Mountain Park Located a few miles east of the city of Atlanta, Stone Mountain rises 825 feet above the 3,200 acres of park land, maintaining an overall elevation of 1,683 feet above sea level. Records indicate that the massive granite dome measures five-miles in circumference and covers 583 acres. The sculptured relief is a three-acre stone memorial to three Civil War heroes: Confederate President Jefferson Davis, Commanding General of the Confederate troops, Robert E. Lee, and Confederate soldier Lt. General Thomas "Stonewall" Jackson. The undertaking spanned a period of fifty-seven years. The carved-figure perspective is greatly distorted due to the great distance between the human eye and the granite figure. The figure of Robert E. Lee reaches the height of a nine-story building, necessary for detail to be seen at such a great distance. Georgia's establishement has an interesting history. British Parliament member Col. James Edward Oglethorpe successfully convinced England's king and Parliament to establish a British Penal Colony for currently imprisoned but nonconvicted men (and their families) who suffered from bad debts and religious persecution. The English jails were overflowing. The colony, named to honor the ruling monarch King George the Second, was established in 1732 and occupied in 1733. *Photo by Robert D. Shangle*

different things as it flows through a number of climates and a variety of landscapes. The headwaters are only a timid little canoe trail, giving no hint of the monster, Olympian river that takes command of the affairs of man and nature in its powerful surge through the entire length of the country. In summer it flows east from Bemidji through a cool green lake-splashed wilderness of rice paddies. This is duck country, with migrating mallards and ringnecks congregating where both wild and cultivated rice and other grains flourish. The upper river, before St. Cloud, is also an avenue through some of Minnesota's vast stands of pine. By the time it passes that city and heads for Minneapolis-St. Paul, it has put away its childish belongings and is giving hints as to what it will become as it moves through the heartland.

Below the Twin Cities, beginning at Lake Pepin, the river is encased in the protective sleeve of the Upper Mississippi River National Wildlife and Fish Refuge for several hundred miles south to Rock Island. Islands in the river are included. Wildlife flourishes in the marshes and on the river bluffs of this sanctuary. Man can actually take credit for some of this influx, especially of the bird species. Dams and locks on this part of the river have stabilized the formerly wide fluctuations in water levels and created marshy habitats for transient bird populations. Atop the high banks, an observer can take in the sinuous curves of the river, visible upstream and down for twenty-five or thirty miles. Wisconsin's hills paint a green and graceful swatch back of the river. Forest, prairie and pastureland combine in a medley of glorious river scenery.

Soon, the immense riches of the upper Midwest begin to find their way to the Mississippi's banks, as towns, built on that wealth, line up downriver: Dubuque, Davenport, Moline, Rock Island, Burlington, Fort Madison, Keokuk, Nauvoo, and Hannibal. The grain of the farmlands of Iowa and Illinois fills the endless parade

Hawaii: 50th State: August 21, 1959—Capital: Honolulu   State Motto: *The life of the land is perpetuated in righteousness.*"
State Bird: Nene   State Flower: Yellow Hibiscus   State Song: "Hawaii Ponoi"   State Tree: Kukui

Pu`uhonua O Honaunau National Historical Park, Honaunau, on the Island of Hawaii Once known as The City of Refuge Park, this site was a haven for protection. The National Park Service states: "…up until the early 19th century, Hawaiians who broke a kapu or one of the ancient laws against the gods could avoid certain death by fleeing to this place of refuge or *pu`uhonua*. The offender would be absolved by a priest and freed to leave. Defeated warriors and noncombatants could also find refuge here during times of battle….The Haloe o Keawe temple and several thatched structures have been reconstructed." Hawaii was first visited by the Spanish in 1555. In 1778 British explorer Captain James Cook arrived and named the islands the Sandwich Islands after his sponsor the Earl of Sandwich. The Hawaiian people ruled these islands under the guidance of the Royal Family until 1898 when the United States annexed the kingdom, removing the Royal command. The United States formally apologized for the overthrow in 1993. The Islands provide an interesting contrast to the other states in the Union. The tropical environment and unique cultural lifestyle has created a strong economy for the state. Pineapple, brought from Spain in 1813, and coffee, first planted in 1818, are leading agricultural crops, along with sugar. The sugar cane plant was present when Captain Cook arrived. *Photo by Shangle Photographics*

of barges bound for Gulf ports. The waters of the river are themselves a bountiful provider, yielding up great quantities of many fish species, including carp and catfish, to commercial and sport fishermen. Opinion is divided as to whether the fishing is better or worse since the upriver dams were constructed, but diversity of opinion is nothing new in a diversity of backgrounds.

It is hard to realize how short a time has passed during the "settling-in" of the river-basin country. The various ethnic strains from the Atlantic seabord—Germans, Scandinavians, Poles, Irish—started to arrive in force in the mid-1800s. Through periods of hard times and prosperity, floods, droughts and crop failures, they have stayed and made the Mississippi Valley the guiding star of the world's farmers. But even before western civilization came, when the river and its domain were entirely creatures of the wild, the region was populated, although thinly, by the Plains Indians—along the upper river, primarily Sioux and Chippewa—when the pioneering settler began to learn of the great Father of Waters. The Native Americans are still there, but the river has changed, or has been changed by the spread of an agricultural and industrial society in contrast to the hunting society. So the Native Americans are no longer the free roamers of the Plains and the undisputed rulers of the river banks.

The river's role as a transportation artery becomes apparent as far north as the Twin Cities. At this point the Mississippi is already a big river, now more sedate and businesslike after the youthful impetuosity and steep descents of its beginnings in the wet wilderness of forested northern Minnesota. After the Falls of St. Anthony at Minneapolis-St. Paul, the Mississippi is forced into mild behavior by over thirty dams and locks strung out all the way to St. Louis, Missouri. But a big change takes place some miles north of St. Louis. The turbulent

Missouri comes in out of the west, practically pushing the main stream aside as it shoulders its way into the channel. For a long while the two rivers keep to their separate channels, the slaty Mississippi following the east bank, the Missouri pouring its turbid stream along the west side. But at Cairo, in the southern corner of Illinois, the giant Ohio adds its tremendous deluge, and from then on the Mississippi takes on its legendary personality. It has become one huge, roiling, tempestuous mud-sculptor of the land. It flows south for another thousand miles in sweeping loops, wandering like a lumbering giant over a broad bed. It never stays long in one place, because as soon as it meets an obstacle, it works powerfully to undercut it. Frequently, the withering river has, in flood time especially, abandoned loops by cutting across their narrow base. The new channel then flows by what has become an oxbow, or horseshoe-shaped lake, created by the powerful current as it digs itself a new bed. These days such events are not as common because control measures have to some extent diminished the Mississippi's power. But Ol' Man River is still dangerous when aroused. At flood times the bottomland along the path of the lower river is still fair game for inundation, despite levees, dams, or diversion channels. The power of the Mississippi can push over or through them, instilling fear and respect of the river into the hearts of men.

Those levees now rise up all along the lower river, sometimes set back a wide space from the banks. On the west bank, they extend from Cape Girardeau, Missouri, and on the east from Cairo, Illinois, running to the Gulf land below New Orleans. The immense wall of one of those man-made wonders, rivaling any earth moving project technology has ever undertaken. The first levees on the river hardly slowed it down when the Mississippi was in flood. They weren't high enough. The present barriers have been penetrated by the river, but the levees have proven to do their job, protecting the land along the river.

Idaho: 43rd State: July 3, 1890—Capital: Boise State Motto: *It is Forever*
State Bird: Mountain Bluebird   State Flower: Syringa   State Song: "Here We Have Idaho"   State Tree: Western White Pine

Mt. McGowan in the Sawtooth National Recreation Area These jagged mountains throughout the region overpower the scene, many of them well over 10,000 feet above sea level. This pristine area is the largest natural wilderness in the United States outside of Alaska. Rich open meadows, white water rivers, clear flowing creeks, and timbered slopes are straight forward descriptions of Idaho's natural grandeur. What is not seen are the agile wild animals that plow across the terrain, the powerful Steelhead that dart through the alpine creeks and rivers, and the available recreational opportunities. Idaho's exploratory history began with the Lewis and Clark Expedition in 1804-1806, crossing through Northern Idaho over the Lolo Pass. Soon fur trappers permeated the area, mingling with the Native Americans (Nez Perce) and establishing settlements. Missionaries arrived, establishing Mission sites and schools, some of which are still operating. Gold and silver mining beckoned miners and are still attracting miners today, as Idaho's economy is soundly supported by the mining industry, as well as tourism. *Photo by Shangle Photographics*

The Lincoln Home, Springfield Abraham Lincoln, with is wife Mary Todd Lincoln, purchased this house in 1844, the only house he ever owned. As their family grew, the house required multiple renovations, developing to a distinctively handsome home. He and his family maintained residence here until 1861 when he took office as the 16th President of the United States and moved to Washington, D. C. The house was rented until 1887 when his son, Robert, donated it to the state of Illinois. Mr. Lincoln was shot and died of an assassin's bullet while in office on April 15, 1865. Lincoln brought much acclaim to Illinois, but the state has much to offer on its own. A colorful Native American history along with fur trappers and French explorers are much of the foundation to the history of Illinois. The railroad changed the economic complexion of the state along with the fact that Illinois has access to the shipping industry via Lake Michigan. This prairie state plays a significant role in the agricultural industry of the nation. *Photo by Robert D. Shangle*

A large measure of the lower river's scenic quality is contained in the bottomlands between the river and the levees. A vast hardwood forest of several million acres grows on these lands, providing quickly renewable timber resources for a big world market. The trees are fast growing, water-tolerant species like cottonwoods, for which a flooding river creates no big problems. On the Mississippi and its tributaries, the cottonwoods of the bank sides thrive and grow into a wood that is both light and tough, with few knots. The rich, wet soil provides ideal conditions for the trees, and a forest can be harvested more than once while other trees in other forests have not yet reached maturity. But these great riverside woodlands also protect abundant wildlife, such as wild turkeys and deer, enriching the area in that way too.

Below St. Louis, the river drops gradually all the way to the Gulf, and river traffic passes freely up and down the river without having to resort to locks. The river of history and legend begins to take over as the water rolls by some celebrated riverbank towns: Memphis, Greenville, Vicksburg, Natchez, and Baton Rouge. The German and Scandinavian accent grows fainter as English, and then French, influence is revealed in the majority of names. The scenery alternates with high, steep cliffs or bluffs with level forest and meadows. Mark Twain (Samuel Clemens) observes in his recollections of the Mississippi River that the river banks from Cairo to the Gulf were mainly unbroken forest in his day. Perched on one of the bluffs is Memphis, the legendary home of the blues. The Memphis names, W. C. Handy and Beale Street, are synonymous with the jazz of both an older and a more recent America.

Arkansas City, much farther south on the west side of the river, is one victim of the capriciousness of the Mississippi. In 1927 it was almost washed away by a great flood on the river. Now the town is high and dry because the river one day decided to move two miles east, leaving Arkansas City with nothing much to do anymore. Not far away, Greenville, Mississippi, communicates with the world of ocean commerce, courtesy of the U.S. Army Corps of Engineers, who in the 1940s succeeded in taming the brutal currents that were eating away at the town's river frontage. Now Greenville is added to the ports that have made another coastline for the moving Mississippi.

The river speaks in whispers of memory, along with the roar of physical power. Ol' Man River flows along the bluffs of Vicksburg, Mississippi, today just as he did during the Civil War, when the town was a Confederate fortress. Vicksburg was the entrance to the western Confederacy and, because of its position on bluffs and surrounded by the river and marshlands, this posed a special problem for attacking Union forces. After some of the war's hardest fighting, General Ulysses S. Grant decided on a siege, which was successful, inflicting a disastrous blow on the Confederacy. In the early twenty-first century, Vicksburg was rescued from the vagaries of the Mississippi, which had succeeded in moving away from the town. Vicksburg is on one of those great river loops that the Mississippi sometimes saws off at the base, making an oxbow lake. Such an event took place in the late 1870s, and for about twenty-five years, Vicksburg was in effect no longer a river port. In 1904 some dredging of the lake opened the southern arm to the Mississippi. The nearby Yazoo River was diverted from the north to flow into the bypassed "lake" to keep the channel open. Vicksburg, again, had access to the Mississippi. The cooperative Yazoo is mild-mannered enough to stir up the lake waters very little, making possible a magnificent harbor for Vicksburg.

The antebellum South is still in evidence in some parts of the Southeast, and so, too, in this Mississippi

Indiana: 19th State: December 11, 1816—Capital: Indianapolis State Motto: *The Crossroads of America*
State Bird: Cardinal   State Flower: Peony   State Song: "On the Banks of the Wabash, Far Away"   State Tree: Tulip

Lincoln Boyhood National Memorial, Lincoln City Referred to as the Lincoln Living Historical Farm, this Spencer County memorial provides a hands-on opportunity to visit a typical dwelling of the 1820's, reminiscent of the time when Abraham Lincoln was living in the immediate area. Daily activities performed by the acting farm-dwellers include the daily chores likely performed by the Lincoln family regarding farming, gardening, tending the farm stock, cooking and performing tasks necessary to provide for the care of the family, such as sewing and quilting. The Memorial Visitor Center has a specific design featuring five-sculpted panels reflecting significant segments of President Lincoln's life. A memorial to Lincoln's mother, Nancy Hanks, is here, as well as her grave site. Indiana history includes such notables as George Rogers Clark, Benjamin Harrison, and Tecumsah. Over ninety covered bridges are scattered throughout the state; significant scenery is provided by the Hocking Hills in southern Indiana. Strategically located in the middle of the industrial and agricultural service center of the nation, highways, airways and railways cross through Indiana. That is the reason Indiana is known as the Crossroads of America. *Photo by Shangle Photographics*

Delta country. Downriver as far as Natchez, in the woods back of the riverside, are some of the extravagant plantation mansions, some quite decayed, some well preserved. Some are deserted, others are lived in, and still others are mere fragments, standing forlorn among the Spanish moss hanging from live oak and cypress trees. Natchez, southernmost of the hilltop river towns, makes a concerted effort to dress itself up as it was in the old days. Restoration of old mansions is a specialty of Natchez, bringing a life again to the city's elegant past.

As the river moves from Natchez toward its southern limits, it seems to become still more restless. Channel maintenance and marking become a job requiring unending vigilance and effort. Not only does the channel shift constantly in the powerful currents, but banks get sucked into the stream in places where it hurls itself against the far side of a bend. Channel and bank markers and lights give added work to the Coast Guard: the river tends to carry them off and reinstall them at locations of its own choosing. In some things the river is still a muscular, muddy mystery, going its own way in spite of man's efforts to tame it with the considerable powers at his command. The Mississippi itself has for a long time been doing its best to reshape the city of Natchez, built both on a hill and on a ledge under the hill by the river. The under-the-hill part, (to quote Mark Twain, was once of "desperate reputation") has been mostly moved downriver, lock, stock, and real estate, by the river currents tearing away at the very ground it stood on.

The river grows wide at Baton Rouge, Louisiana, rolling grandly through a broad valley of farming country until it reaches New Orleans. The levees, up to forty feet high, follow its curving path all the way, for some mighty floods have washed over the lower river delta land. Baton Rouge is no longer just the epitome of Twain's "absolute South." The author remembers it as "clothed in flowers." That is not untrue today, although it

Iowa: 29th State: December 28, 1846—Capital: Des Moines State Motto: *Our liberties we prize and our rights we will maintain.*
State Bird: Eastern Goldfinch   State Flower: Wild Rose   State Song: "The Song of Iowa"   State Tree: Oak

Amana Colonies, east-central Iowa   Seven small villages provide communal centers for the people of the Amana Church Society: Amana, East Amana, Middle Amana, High Amana, West Amana, South Amana, and Homestead. It was 1844 when some 800 members of the Ebenezer Society arrived in Iowa from New York, taking residence on the 18,000 acres that had been purchased as a new community location. Their secure, devoted and private lives are still achieved, however with modern changes. The Amana Society is now recognized as a national leader in several manufacturing industries. France first laid claim to the Iowa land in 1673 by Jesuit priest Jacque Marquette and French Canadian explorer Louis Jolliet while searching for the Mississippi River. The land was acquired by the United States through the Louisiana Purchase of 1803. Wide spread farming denotes Iowa as a state that feeds the nation. *Photo by Robert D. Shangle*

Kansas: 34th State: January 29, 1861—Capital: Topeka State Motto: *To the Stars through Difficulties*
State Bird: Western Meadowlark   State Flower: Sunflower   State Song: "Home on the Range"   State Tree: Cottonwood

The Eisenhower Center, Abilene Dwight David Eisenhower, 34th President of the United States of America, lived in Abilene from 1892 until he entered the United States Military Academy in 1911. His career as a soldier began as a Second Lieutenant in the Army, working up to the Supreme Commander of Allied Forces and General of the Army. He retired from active duty in 1952 and was elected President of the United States, taking the oath of office on January 20, 1953 and again for a second term on January 20, 1957. He died March 28, 1969 in Washington, D. C. He and his wife, Mamie, are buried in the Place of Meditation at the Eisenhower Center. The old Eisenhower family first arrived in Abilene country in 1878-1879, having purchased land from Kansas Pacific Railroad. The railroad made a major impact on the importance of Kansas and to Abilene, as the railroad provided the way to get the cattle to market. Today cattle are vitally important to Kansas, along with such agricultural crops as corn, sorghum, soybeans and wheat. *Photo by Robert D. Shangle*

doesn't go far enough. Modern Baton Rouge wears an outer garment of oil refineries and chemical plants, sitting as it does in the center of the rich oil fields of the Gulf region. One of the main concerns now on this stretch of the Mississippi is control of the great volume of pollutants that are the inevitable bequest of the widespread industrialization along the river's lower reaches.

A very grand finale, indeed, to the Mississippi's 2,400-mile odyssey is the city of New Orleans. It is not quite the end of the trip, because the sea is still about one-hundred miles away, pushed back by the river's delta, building out into the Gulf of Mexico. But if not a finale, New Orleans is certainly a crowning point. New Orleans is preeminent in human affairs as a city of life, a stimulating place to be. All of the senses come to attention there. Taste is one. Dining can be high-quality French cooking, but also variations of the more earthy Cajun and Creole dishes that combine seafood, rice, and other common ingredients into extraordinary, gastronomical experiences.

New Orleans is one of the country's biggest ports, and one of the lowest-lying ports. The riverbank levees have been built up to such a height that the immense volume of Gulf and river shipping is invisible from town. But it is there, floating on a river whose surface overtops the land. New Orleaners must feel more secure behind their earthen walls now than they used to, especially if they have read Samuel Clemens' description of it all. He felt called upon to record, in regard to the levee, that "there is nothing but that frail breastwork of earth between the people and destruction."

This is not a book about cities. Its photographs reflect the grandeur and the glory and the variety of a continent-wide landscape. But cities like New Orleans have a kind of magic that makes them seem a very

Fort Boonesborough State Park, near Richmond   The Fort was established in 1775 by Richard Henderson and Daniel Boone. Daniel Boone is credited for locating what is known as the Cumberland Gap, an opening through the mountainous terrain that allowed travel from the southeast for western expansion. Fort Boonesborough, southeast of Lexington, provided service to travelers and locals for some fifty years. Reconstructed buildings provide an insight to historical activities of the time. Kentucky has a varied terrain from mountainous in the east to rounded hills in the north. Much of the state is forested land. The heart of the state is referred to as Bluegrass Country, made famous by the demonstrated equestrian strength so obvious to the area. Lexington refers to itself as the "Horse Capital of the World." Kentucky and the Derby go hand-in-glove along with Churchill Downs, the center of Horse Racing activities in Louisville. Kentucky is rich in agriculture production, such as corn, soybeans, and burley tobacco; in raising livestock: cattle, hogs, sheep, and chicken, with particular emphasis on horses and mules. *Photo by Shangle Photographics*

natural part of that landscape, even with high-rise buildings and super domes. They have grown up making a contribution to their natural endowment, a contribution that may be too subtle for the physical eye or the logical mind. Sometimes it is a *felt* thing more than anything else. New Orleans may really be an attitude more than a physical presence, though it has plenty of the latter. It sums up the lower Mississippi Basin by being not only its main mover and shaper in an economic sense, but also by keeping its ties with a creative past and, by building on that past, a new level of accomplishment that makes its future as a vibrant living place assured.

No matter that the Mississippi today is hidden behind the levees and wharves of New Orleans. The river is not so wide, as it bends past the city, as some lesser rivers become when they get near the end of the trail. But it is deep, very deep—about one-hundred feet in mid-channel. The Mississippi seems to be returning to its beginnings in its powerful and silt-laden surge past the big port city and on to its rendezvous with the Gulf. It still flows like a river, even though there are only a few more mile to go. It is not saying to the waiting sea, "Well, here I am, I've had it." No, the mystery is still intact, the muscle is still there as it pours powerfully into the Gulf. The river keeps building more land as if it needs to keep on going, to turn the Gulf into one more riverside lake. Maybe it will keep on building until it can challenge the Congo and the Amazon for the title of world's greatest river.

Our Golden West

Somewhere out on the Great Plains, Midwest becomes West: you feel it in Wyoming and Montana, and you know it for a fact in Texas and Oklahoma. What you feel and how you know is difficult to say—the land looks the same, but the sum of dozens of intangibles suddenly adds up to something different than it did in Minneapolis or Des Moines. The land itself makes a spectacular commitment to that difference in the form of the Rocky Mountains on its rugged way to the Pacific Ocean…and beyond, to the western strongholds of Alaska and Hawaii.

It is quite remarkable that terrain as different as the Plains and the massive mountains of the western third of the nation could exist so close to each other. Yet the Plains would certainly not be the Plains without the contributions of soil layers from the Rockies over millions of years. And our respect for the Rockies can only be increased by the fact that we have the Plains from which to look at them. There can be few sights to equal the Front Range, that awesome face of the Shining Mountains that soars abruptly from the western edge of the Colorado Plain.

The relatively young Rocky Mountain Range is scenarist and stage director for the western scenic drama. We are told that the present mountain mass is not the first version to ornament the North American continent. Well, even if they are only second-growth mountains, they are a bona fide national treasure and the object of endless admiration. The Rockies of the United States stretch through Montana, Wyoming, Colorado,

Louisiana: 18th State: April 30, 1812—Capital: Baton Rouge   State Motto: *Union, Justice and Confidence*

State Bird: Eastern Brown Pelican   State Flower: Magnolia   State Song: "Give Me Louisiana"   State Tree: Cypress

Jackson Square in the French Quarter, New Orleans   At the heart of the French Quarter, the St. Louis Cathedral dominates the Square once the center of military and government activities; today it is a gathering place of visitor activities. The huge bronze statue honors General Andrew Jackson, the victorious commander of the Battle of New Orleans. French explorer Sieur de La Salle took possession of the land as he descended the Mississippi River in 1682, naming the country Louisiana in honor of King Louis XIV. Ownership transferred between France and Spain, then England and back to France who then sold the land known as the Louisiana Purchase to the United States in 1803. The city of New Orleans began about 1718, Shreveport was founded in 1837 and the first Mardi Gras parade was held in New Orleans on Shrove Tuesday. The state of Louisiana reports that the state is a national leader in growing cotton, sugarcane, rice, sweet potatoes, pecans, soybeans and corn, and livestock product includes poultry, dairy and beef cattle. " Louisiana is the nation's largest producer of alligator hides and crawfish." The tourism industry is easily a state economy leader since historical sites and points of interest prevail throughout the state. *Photo by Robert D. Shangle*

Maine: 23rd State: March 15, 1820—Capital: Augusta   State Motto: *I direct.*

State Bird: Chickadee   State Flower: State Song: "State Song of Maine"   State Tree: White Pine Cone and Tassel

Portland Head Light, Portland Harbor/Casco Bay near Cape Elizabeth at Fort Williams Park   Maine's oldest lighthouse was lighted in 1791 and automated in 1989. Still maintaining an active status, the eighty-foot tower gained a Keepers Quarters in 1891, which today includes a gift shop and interpretive museum. There are over sixty lighthouses along the Maine coastline giving mariner aid to vessels out in the Atlantic Ocean. The rocky coast of Maine was first explored by England's designate explorers John Cabot and his son Sebastian in 1498-1499 under the guidance of King Henry VII. The French arrived and then the English. This New England state borders Canada on the upper northwest, north and northeast, while the Atlantic Ocean edges Maine's southern shore; New Hampshire is directly west. This is a land covered with lakes, rivers and streams, beckoning the adventuresome sportsman who loves to hunt, fish and investigate the backwoods locales. *Photo by Shangle Photographics*

New Mexico, and the western tip of Texas to the Mexican border. They dribble over into the neighboring states of Idaho, Utah, and Arizona, where they are known, in part, as the Bitterroots, the Wasatch Range, and the San Francisco Peaks of north-central Arizona.

Apparently the Plains Indians were more or less content to worship the Shining Mountains from afar, rarely venturing into their rugged interior. Even the obsessive push of the American pioneers, though it surmounted this barrier, could not really conquer it: this invasion, and the later one of gold and silver, affected only the lower fringes of the mountain-and-forest wilderness. These days, some of the range's most spectacular configurations are set aside as preserves, such as those in Glacier, Yellowstone, and Rocky Mountain National Parks.

Even in the twentieth century, man has not been able to take the edge of the wilderness off the Rockies. To be sure, there are roads through the mountains now, however most Americans stay on them. Trails that begin where the asphalt covering stops are left to the more adventuresome and rugged of us, those who are on speaking terms with bears and snakes and such. Launching out into the great unknown of a pure wilderness is something that we may think about in our less rational moments, but common sense usually comes to our rescue before we get to the point of acting on these wild impulses. Yet there is no wilderness experience from a car. We can say "we were there" if we drive along the Yellowstone Park roads. But the most complete wilderness experiences are usually away from the roads, out of sight, and we have to work to attain them. Far from the paved roads are the jewel-like blue lakes lying within soaring mountain walls that seem to reach to infinity; idyllic mountain meadows filled with softly waving grasses or brilliant with multicolored spring wildflowers, all blushing quite unseen over a snowy ridge somewhere.

Esthetic appreciation of nature has always been a pastime of man, but in years past it has taken back seat to "appreciation" of a more practical kind: mining, logging, and constructing dams and powerhouses. But the key word in a statement like that is "practical," and it has been encouraging in the past few decades to see that the definition of practicality is being expanded.

Commentators discussing the Native Americans tell us with assurance that the various tribes living in this land had no idea of the wealth hidden in the rivers, on the plains, or in the mountains. Indeed, one might wonder which of the things that we have would be counted as riches by the Indians: they lived as hunters, or practiced a minimal sort of agriculture. Since the time European civilization spread over this continent, we have taken little note of the influence of the Native American in our thoughts and in our way of life. But it seems to me that his example of closeness to nature and care in his relations with it has finally penetrated our national consciousness. The rest of us are beginning to think it might not be so bad to live with nature rather than in spite of it.

Rivers are the shapers of the earth, even if they all do their jobs a little bit differently. We have seen how the waterways of the Midwest, with their vast water volumes and low gradients, chew away constantly at their banks and pile up great barriers of sediment, wandering erratically over beds as much as eighty-miles wide. The western rivers are different. They dig into the earth rather than wander over it (except in flood time). The gentle slope from the High Plains to the Mississippi River is not duplicated on the western side of the Rockies. Here such fast-moving streams as the Colorado, the Green, the Rio Grande, the Pecos, the Snake, Salmon, and Columbia drop down from mountain heights in a frantic rush, speaking in a characteristic roar as they hurry

Maryland: 7th State: April 28, 1788—Capital: Annapolis   State Motto: *Manly Deeds, Womanly Words*

State Bird: Baltimore Oriole   State Flower: Black-eyed Susan   State Song: "Maryland, My Maryland"   State Tree: White Oak

Fort McHenry National Monument and Historic Shrine, Baltimore   Built between 1798 and 1803, Fort McHenry, restored to pre-Civil War condition, was an active military facility through World War II (1945). During the battle for control of Baltimore (War of 1812), thirty-five year old poet-lawyer Francis Scott Key penned the words to the national anthem, "The Star Spangled Banner," as he viewed the American flag flying victoriously from the Fort. By presidential proclamation the flag now flies twenty-four hours a day, at the exact location as it was on September 14, 1814. The state of Maryland is considered a Mid-Atlantic state, stretching from the Atlantic Ocean to the Allegheny Mountains in the northwest. The huge Chesapeake Bay provides a unique specialness to Maryland. From North to South the Bay is 195-miles long, allowing ocean-going vessels to reach the Port of Baltimore, established in 1706, and "has grown to become one of the busiest ports on the East Coast of the United States." *Photo by James Blank*

between cliffs and over rocky boulders, creating turbulent flowing water that plunges over the abrupt edge of the earth into marvelous appearing waterfalls of all sizes. They are more glittery than their slower moving eastern kin.

The star of the canyon cutters is the Colorado River. The Colorado's masterwork is so stupendous that it has swallowed up its creator. The Grand Canyon of the Colorado is not quite the world's deepest canyon (Hells Canyon on the Snake River between Idaho and Oregon has that distinction: 7,800 ft), but its extent—about 200 miles—and the intricate carving of multi-hued rock as the river winds a swift, grinding course over its floor, assure its supremacy as the most spectacular cleft in the earth's surface. The canyon is a monument to the earth's powerful forces, internal and external, acting in conjunction with each other over millions of years. The Colorado, cutting down, is like all streams, attempting to reach sea level; the high Kaibab Plateau keeps pushing up, now generally more than a mile above the river. Presumably the river will keep cutting down until it reaches is absolute level, and the plateau keeps rising. Who is to say if the Grand Canyon may not one day be even more grand.

With the Colorado's vast hole in the ground as a superb example, the variety of our scenic West is one of its most noteworthy aspects. Plunging canyons are just as inspiring as high, glaciated mountain ranges. So, to, the "badlands" of the West—the deserts and eroded wastes that cover many square miles in parts of all the states west of the Rocky Mountains. The rivers and the winds are the primary sculptors for the stark, weirdly designed rock formations found in parts of the Southwest. Utah's Zion and Bryce canyons, with their Arches and Canyonlands National Parks, are among the most extensive of these phenomena. Zion, with its gigantic, brilliantly colored monoliths carved by the little Virgin River, seems like a series of sculptures that took on a life of their own after they outgrew their creator. Bryce's battalions of colorful limestone and sandstone rock fantasies

Massachusetts: 6th State: February 6, 1788—Capital: Boston State Motto: *By the sword we seek peace, but peace only under liberty*
State Bird: Chickadee   State Flower: Mayflower   State Song: "Hail Massachusetts"   State Tree: American Elm

Rockport Harbor at Rockport on Cape Ann The charm of Rockport began back in 1690. Today the active fishing fleet moves in-and-out of the small harbor, listing itself as one of the many fishing fleets that ply the Atlantic waters off the state of Massachusetts. Nearby is Gloucester, America's oldest seaport, settled in 1623, one of the busiest seaports on the Eastern seacoast. Early American history permeates all of Massachusetts beginning with the arrival of the Pilgrims on the *Mayflower* at Plymouth Rock; the historical events in and around Boston, Salem, and Marblehead. There is huge Cape Cod with the settlement of Provincetown, the success at the Marconi Station, and the interest on the southern shore vacation land have prevailed. From the jagged coastline and flat lands of the east, the land rises to gentle hill country in the west. *Photo by Robert D. Shangle*

Michigan: 26th State: January 16, 1837—Capital: Lansing   State Motto: *If you seek a pleasant peninsula, look about you*
State Bird: Robin   State Flower: Apple Blossom   State Song: "Michigan, My Michigan"   State Tree: White Pine

Mackinac Island, Lake Huron Island guests enjoy the manicured-green that sweeps the island's grounds down to the marina on the shore of Lake Huron, one of the five Great Lakes within the United States. A leisure cruise over the waters of Lake Huron and Lake Michigan can provide an exhilarating experience. The pace of life is definitely slower here, as no automobiles are allowed on the island. A horse-drawn carriage is available for touring the three-mile long by two-mile-wide island. Bicycle tours and the old-fashioned walking tour is a quiet approach to island exploration. The remarkable Grand Hotel, debuting in 1887, is a grand centerpiece to the island's history. Michigan has two sections: the Upper Peninsula, which is a sportsman's paradise and a natural wonder, and the Lower Peninsula where centers of industry produce and manufacture products used world wide. The automobile industry is a leading producer in Michigan's economy, along with a wide variety of agriculture products, such a cherries, peaches and blueberries. The mining industry reaches deep into the Upper Peninsula's development. *Photo by Shangle Photographics*

on a pink and white base have an eerie resemblance to a haunted city whose inhabitants are in a state of suspended animation. Arches and Canyonlands National Parks, specializing in great, soaring rock bridges and "windows," show the scouring effects of wind and other natural sculptors. Here, too, the Colorado River has been in the canyon-making business, combining with the Green River to chisel deep pathways through Utah's vast limestone plateau.

These barren rock terrains of the plateau country possess a kind of unearthly beauty whose grandeur is undeniable. The sharply etched canyons and rock structures seem to be involved in a time warp, projecting a raw, youthful earth unsoftened by time. The deserts of the West have this stark aspect, too, of course. But calling them wastelands in the same sense as the plateau and canyon country would not be quite accurate. Some of them are deeply covered with fertile soil, deposited when they were lake bottoms in a previous geological age. The Colorado Desert of California is certainly one of these fertile but arid basins. Here the Imperial and Coachella valleys, watered by giant irrigation canals from the Colorado River, grow enormous volumes of fruit, produce and grains.

The biggest desert in the United States spreads over the Great Basin, between the Sierra Nevada and the Wasatch Range. It is not by any means a desert of uniform aspect or climate, including latitudinal ranges and topography that is as varied as desert can be. The Great Basin deserts are generally high, but include the lowest point in the United States: 280 feet below sea level in Death Valley. California's Mojave Desert is considered closely related, if not actually a part of them. Most of Nevada is included, and parts of Utah, Wyoming, Idaho and Oregon. The other big desert, the Arizona-Sonora, spreads over southern Arizona and into the Mexican

Split Rock Lighthouse, Lake Superior   Perched atop a 130-foot bluff overlooking Lake Superior, Split Rock Lighthouse began its operational career in 1910 and continued until 1969. The demand for a lighthouse for this area came about following the loss and damage of some twenty-nine ships during the November 28, 1905, blizzard and gale. Considered by many to be one of the more picturesque locations on the Great Lakes, the lighthouse was featured on a U. S. postage stamp issued in 1995. The lighthouse is located within the 100 acre Split Rock Lighthouse State Park. Minnesota is the land of Hiawatha, the Ojibwe Indian Brave immortalized by Henry Wadsworth Longfellow's *Song of Hiawatha* and to legendary lumberjack Paul Bunyon and his Blue Ox Babe. The Northern Prairie Wildlife Research Center states: "...the state of Minnesota has more than 15,000 lakes; 63,000 miles of natural rivers and streams; 23,000 miles of drainage ditches and channelized watercourses; and more than 10 million acres of wetlands, including peatlands, marshes, sloughs, brushy swamps, forested lowlands, and wet meadows." *Photo by Shangle Photographics*

state of Sonora. The biggest desert cacti—the Saguaro and Organ Pipe—are almost exclusively limited to this desert.

What is most fascinating about the deserts is the abundance of beautiful and wonderful life forms they support. Rainfall, or the lack of it, determines how exuberant the life will be. After a relatively damp winter, the springtime desert explodes into a brilliant bloom, a veritable medley of colors, short-lived but sensational. And the animal populations are also diverse, including reptilian adaptations such as the sidewinder. Snakes in the desert depend on the rodent population at mealtime, and the deserts are well supplied in this respect. The desert fox does a big business on the desert rabbit. Hawks and eagles give him some stiff competition as they fly sorties over the burning sands, rocks, and sagebrush in the hope of scaring up a meal. Smaller birds, such as vireos and wrens, find perches from whence they can concentrate on insects and seeds. Even at night in the desert, creatures are stirring. Hunted animals are on the move, then, confident of the protection of darkness; hunters are out, too, ready to pounce on some unwary mouse.

The western deserts come to an end at a high barrier not far from the edge of the continent: the Cascade Range of the Northwest and the Sierra Nevada of California. These long north-south mountains are among the tallest and most rugged of our ranges. The slopes of the Cascades support vast forests of fir and pine, with lesser stands of spruce and cedar. The Cascades are characterized by distinct peaks, separate volcanic cones that carry gigantic glaciers and tower over the land, their summits sometimes visible for a hundred miles in all directions. Great freestanding mountains like Rainier, Hood and Shasta are not only awesome in bulk and beauty, but also in their ability to create their own weather, as often as not sticking their heads and shoulders into clouds of their own making. They are mountain climber's mountains, offering glacial challenges to all comers. Washington's North Cascades, especially, cluster together in such a wild and rugged jumble of mountains and glaciers that only the hardiest and most resourceful wilderness hikers venture into their primitive interior.

The mighty wall of the Sierra constitutes a more coherent range than the Cascades. Wholly within California, it features several peaks above 14,000 feet, including Mt. Whitney, highest point in the United States outside of Alaska. The Sierra Nevada almost single-handedly makes California what it is and the range has played an important role in the history of our westward expansion. Donner Pass, the northward crossing of the range, achieved notoriety as the site of the ill-fated winter crossing of the Donner party in 1847. The frantic California gold rush was centered mainly in the western foothills of the Sierra, and many towns today, such as Oroville and Placerville, have names and histories that bear witness to those times. The Sierra's unusual light-colored granite and fantastic glacial scouring have given them some of the most breathtaking rock structures of any mountain system. The best known of these areas is Yosemite Valley in Yosemite National Park. The Valley seems to have been built especially as a seat for the gods. The Merced River (with some glacial help) has made a unique scenic extravaganza of Yosemite.

The Cascades have their share of the fascinating and the fabulous. One of these phenomena is Crater Lake in southern Oregon. Now a national park, the lake is situated in the crater of a high volcano that was once a much higher one, known as Mt. Mazama, before it blew its top long ago. Rain water and melting snows have created the lake, which has no outlet. Crater Lake with a depth of 1,932 feet, is among the deepest in the world, but it is famous for other things as well as depth. The lake's surface has an intense blue color (depending on the

Mississippi: 20th State: December 10, 1817—Capital: Jackson State Motto: *By Valor and Arms*
State Bird: Mockingbird   State Flower: Magnolia   State Song: "Go Mississippi"   State Tree: Magnolia

The Historic Stanton House, Natchez Built in 1857 on an entire city block, the Stanton House is one of many antebellum mansions that grace the historic sections of Natchez, the oldest civilized settlement on the Mississippi River. The river creates a natural boundary on the west, the state of Louisiana and the Gulf of Mexico are on the south, and the state of Alabama is the east boundary. The climate is semitropical, which provides for a long growing season. Cotton is still the leading agricultural product along with soybeans, catfish and rice, while manufacturing is the principal economic activity, supported by livestock, forestry, mining and tourism. A colorful history laces through the entire state, which includes nostalgic early settlement history by the French, British, Spanish, and early American penetration. The Civil War had a great impact on Mississippi, a Confederate state, leaving evidence of its presence throughout the state. *Photo by James Blank*

Missouri: 24th State: August 10, 1821—Capital: Jefferson City   State Motto: *The Welfare of the People shall be the Supreme Law*

State Bird: Bluebird   State Flower: Hawthorn   State Song: "Missouri Waltz"   State Tree: Flowering Dogwood

The University of Missouri-Columbia at Columbia   Founded in 1839, the columns of Old Academic Hall, which was destroyed by fire in 1892, stand as the focal point of Francis Quadrangle on the University's Columbia campus, one of four campus sites within the system. In 1843 a three-hour commencement ceremony was held for the first graduating class comprised of two students. Women were admitted for the first time in 1868. Missouri is a frontier state steeped in history: Native American history; the arrival of the French-Canadians investigating the hunting and mining opportunities; followed by the inquiring settlers making their way to new frontiers. The Lewis and Clark Expedition paved the way for western movers. As more people arrived, the railroads moved in-and-through the Missouri landscape. Mining exploration came into its own, and in 1870 the Missouri School of Mines and Metallurgy was founded. Mining and farming have been important economic factors since settlers first arrived on the scene. The lovely rolling hills and fertile plains north of the Missouri River are in stark contrast to the rough hills and deep narrow valleys of the land south of the river. *Photo by Robert D. Shangle*

weather) that seems quite unreal. And the steep walls of the volcano that contain the lake give it a setting unmatched anywhere in the world.

The coastal mountain ranges, all the way from the Olympics in Washington state to the Peninsular Ranges of Southern California, present a nearly continuous wall where the continent meets the Pacific Ocean. They are not all lined up at the water's edge, but where they are, as in Oregon and Northern California, the coastal profile becomes a line of sculptured cliffs and headlands of surpassing beauty. In some place, enormous, wild promontories reach far out into the Pacific Ocean, rising majestically from the foaming waves as if defying them to do their worst. At other places along the coast, the mountains stand back a bit. Here they reach out to the waters with their skirts, so to speak, and the savage ocean has torn at the land to create great perpendicular bluffs and bays of intricate design. In still other parts of the Pacific shoreline, the mountains have temporarily retired from the coast, and wide, white sandy beaches dip at a gentle slope into the welcoming sea. But, except for the Southern California beaches and a small bay here and there, the welcome is a chilly one for would-be bathers. Where the Pacific meets the shore, its waters are only for those with insulated skin. Both commercial and sport fishing are big industries off the Pacific Coast: there are plenty of fish in the sea, cold waters or not.

Farther West

Not very long ago, when people had arrived on the Pacific side after a trip from the East Coast, they could say they had traveled across the whole country. Nowadays the country reaches much farther to the northwest and the southeast. Alaska and Hawaii give the United States a global reach. Parts of Alaska, the biggest state, and all of Hawaii, the most volcanic of the states, are so far west in position that they are almost Far East. Alaska, of course, is very much a part of the North American continent. The Aleutian archipelago, coming so close to the Asian mainland, almost seems to be trying to get away, so far is its reach into the Bering Sea. The farthest island is indeed east of the International Date Line.

Alaska and Hawaii are as wildly different, superficially at least, as anything we have managed to put together in the rest of the country. Even though the whole of Alaska is certainly not north of the Arctic Circle, enough of it is to make its ice a self-renewing resource. Most of Hawaii—the main island group—is south of the Tropic of Cancer, so it is better at making fire than ice. But everybody knows these days, if they ever thought otherwise, that Alaska is not one big ice field. Since the forty-ninth state joined up, and since the Prudhoe Bay oil fields began sending crude oil through the big pipeline to Valdez, Alaska has been publicized as it never was before. We have been deluged with information about the unbelievable natural resources of that north land. We know about the immense areas being set aside as preserves, to protect them from development. Alaska, after all, has more of everything than almost anyplace else. So some of it should be put into preserves and remain as wilderness.

Space is the first thing that comes to mind in regard to what Alaska has. And now more of us know that its 356-million acres come in many forms and with a variety of weather systems. Some specifics may escape us. For instance its coastline. Alaska has more of it than all the rest of the United States. The Tongass National Forest on the narrow panhandle west of Canada is the largest federal forest in the nation. Alaska's glaciers and ice

Montana: 41st State: November 8, 1889—Capital: Helena State Motto: *Gold and Silver*
State Bird: Western Meadowlark   State Flower: Bitterroot   State Song: "Montana"   State Tree: Ponderosa Pine

Lower Medicine Lake and Rising Wolf Mountain, Glacier National Park This spectacular scene is in Glacier National Park in Montana's Rocky Mountains. Some fifty active glaciers still work the earth in Glacier National Park, and about 200 lakes and countless creeks and streams beckon the fisherman; over thirty mountain peaks soar past 7,000 feet and up to 10,000 feet. Passing over the Continental Divide can go unnoticed unless the flow of the water catches your eye. As an imaginary line along the peaks of the Rockies, it is apparent that the water-flow divides: west towards the Pacific and east towards the Gulf of Mexico. The western third of Montana is breathtaking beauty of mountains and forested scenic vistas; the eastern two-thirds is gently rolling land that creates the Great Plains. Two major rivers cut through Montana, moving in an eastern destination: the Missouri and the Yellowstone. Lewis and Clark explored Montana during their 1804-1806 expedition, preceded by the French who first arrived in 1742. As time past Indians and invading settlers clashed, best remembered by the Battle of the Little Big Horn in 1876. Copper, gold, silver and zinc mining was instrumental in the economic development of Montana, along with the railroad. *Photo by Shangle Photographics*

fields are the largest on earth; anyone who has taken an Inside Passage trip through those fjord-like Panhandle waters, or watched the shoreline of Prince William Sound from the deck of a pleasure cruiser knows how awesome and accessible those glaciers are as they come sliding down to the sea. And Alaska has some close affinities, too, with Hawaii. The weather is quite mild many days of the year— even hot once in awhile— in the southeastern and south-central regions. And as Hawaii has some dynamic volcanics, so has Alaska. That was in the Alaska Peninsula's Valley of Ten Thousand Smokes in 1910 when Katmai Volcano coughed up a truly cosmic volume of ash—215 cubic miles north. So Alaska, like Hawaii, is part of the Pacific's "ring of fire," where volcanism is ever present.

Hawaii is tiny by comparison with Alaska: only 6,415-square miles as compared to 586,000 for the big north land. However, the Hawaiian Islands is several times more populated than Alaska. Each of the seven main inhabited islands—Oahu, Maui, Hawaii, Kauai, Molokai, Niihau and Lanai—has maintained much of their natural tropical beauty. All of the Hawaiian Islands are volcanoes, and the largest of the islands, Hawaii, is the youngest of the chain and still in an active classification. Kilauea, a crater on the slopes of Mauna Loa in Hawaii Volcanoes National Park, sometimes belches fiery red lava in various hot spots on its flanks. The Hawaii Center for Volcanology states that "ongoing eruption has produced a broad field of new lava flows that have buried over 102 sq km of the volcano's south flank and added more than 205 hectares (560 acres) of new land to the island." The lava flow has destroyed several communities, including scores of homes and other buildings, and historical sites.

One obvious reason Hawaii is such an attractive people place is the benign climate, freshened constantly

Nebraska: 37th State: March 1, 1867—Capital: Lincoln State Motto: *Equality before the Law*
State Bird: Western Meadowlark   State Flower: Goldenrod   State Song: "Beautiful Nebraska"   State Tree: Cottonwood

Scotts Bluff National Monument, Scottsbluff This 800-foot bluff was a looming landmark for the weary traveler on the Oregon Trail who looked for guidance across the rolling prairie land. Other major landmarks east of the Monument along the North Platte are Chimney Rock National Historic Site, Courthouse Rock and Jail Rock, and Ash Hollow (the site of the river crossing). The historical trek across the Great Plains along the Oregon Trail began in 1843. Several thousand people and animals would pass by strategic locations, such as Fort Kearny, on a daily basis. At the time Nebraska was a passing-through area, but some of the travelers became aware of the rich grassland that was being past over. They set down roots and began farming. Today, Nebraska's farmers grow abundant amounts of corn, sorghum, soybeans, hay, wheat, beans, oats, potatoes and sugar beets. The Missouri River is the state boundary on the east, running through the major city of Omaha. The wide, meandering Platte River joins the Missouri just south of Omaha. *Photo by Robert D. Shangle*

The Red Rock Canyon National Conservation Area near Las Vegas   Here is a living desert of unusual scenery and just one of many beautiful spots in the inquisitive state of Nevada. Though its chief economic producer is gaming, there is much more to see in Nevada than cards, dice, extravaganza musicals and glittering lights. There is the Cowboy Country of the north, which many consider to be the last outpost of the real American West. There are the wide open spaces referred to as the Pioneer Country, where wild horses, burros, antelope and elk roam freely; there are ghost towns and archaeological dig sites to visit. The Lake Tahoe area provides natural wonderment, both summer and winter, and is the gateway to Carson City and Reno. Southern Nevada is open, flat and dry, making way to Lake Mead, the largest man-made lake in the country. Hoover Dam completed in 1935 holds back the water of the Colorado River behind a dam that is 727 feet high. Nearby is Boulder City, where gambling is not allowed, and Las Vegas, where gambling makes the city. *Photo by Shangle Photographics*

by warm trade winds out of the east and northeast. Lowland Hawaii has no winter, or any seasons at all except summer. Honolulu temperatures during the winter months have an average range from 65° to 80°, while in the summer the lows and highs are in the 70° to 80° range. Things are a bit chillier in the more mountainous parts, but except for Maui's Haleakala at 10,000 feet and 13,000-foot-plus domes of Mauna Loa and Muana Kea on the Big Island, the high points top off at about 5,000 feet. Some islands and some places on the same island are wetter than others. Kauai's Waialeale Peak averages 460 inches of rain a year. Other island locations receive twenty inches or less.

Some of the variations among the Islands have to do with their relative age. Kauai, one of the oldest, has the softest, greenest landscape. Its long-dormant volcano is clothed in lush foliage that softens the flanks of its deep, rain cut gorges. Kauai's famous Na Pali coast is an isolated sanctuary where immense rugged cliffs plunge into the sea and cut off access by land. Oahu, the most populated, has many good swimming beaches. West Maui, too, has lots of sandy beaches and the haunting steep-walled Iao Valley that is clothed in green. The Big Island next door has its volcanic country, grasslands and valleys in its interior that contrast sharply with that stark terrain. The waters around the Islands are glassy-clear, colorful coral jungles, where skin divers can go exploring among the blizzard of fish life that gathers there.

Hawaii and Alaska's fascination extends beyond the merely physical. Both states have colorful history, contributing to their mystique. Alaska was the goal of hordes of fortune-seekers during the Gold Rush of the 1880s. Hawaii's Lahaina on Maui has the distinction of royalty and the notoriety as a busy and prosperous whaling port. New England sent both whalers and missionaries to this free-wheeling town.

73

The Albany Bridge in the White Mountains The bridge, originally built in 1858, spans the Swift River, known as one of the finest whitewater rivers in New England. The precipitous river drops more than 2,400 feet in elevation over a twenty-six mile distance between Livermore and Albany before joining the Saco River in Conway. Native American history is sustained by such mountain names as Passaconaway (Child of the Bear), Kancamagus (The Fearless One), and Paugus (The Oak), easily viewed from Kancamagus Highway, designated a Scenic Byway through the White Mountains. New Hampshire was a planned settlement by the English, established as a fishing colony at the mouth of the Piscataqua River, and one of the original thirteen colonies. It is bounded on the west by the Connecticut River, on the north by Canada, on the east by Maine and the Atlantic Ocean, on the south by Massachusetts, and on the west by Vermont. Its overall length is about 180 miles and its width varies from 50 to a maximum of 93 miles. Manufacturing, tourism, and agriculture are principal industries throughout the state. *Photo by Shangle Photographics*

Our Mellow and Mountainous East

The eastern United States, at least the part that started us on our career as a nation, is in many ways the center of culture and tradition for the country. Citizens who reside outside of the original thirteen colonies sometimes take offense at that assumption, but the east is, to be sure, almost a separate civilization from other regions. To some extent, this phenomenon has to do with age: just as England and Europe have acquired a certain sophisticated world view that escapes Americans in general, so the East, with its 200 years on the rest of the country, speaks a language that can be both irksome and instructive to other Americans.

Actually, age is just about all that Easterners can claim in common: the Atlantic Seaboard states admit to very few generalities otherwise. Maine is not much like Massachusetts in appearance or style; Connecticut, New York and Maryland are not similar to each other, or any other place, either; the Old South and the New South exist side by side in places that have had strong local identities for over 300 years. And southernmost is Florida, where St. Augustine was a going concern of the Spanish some fifty-five years before the Pilgrim Fathers landed at Plymouth. To a great extent, Florida is a world of its own.

The length of American history in this area is complemented by the mellow, old look that clothes the countryside. The coastal belt and the states immediately west are, allowing for the coastal plains, wrapped in some of the world's oldest mountains. The soft outlines of their forested slopes suggested ease and stability.

The long Appalachian chain rises in Alabama and Georgia and sweeps north over a wide path, passing deep inland in the area of the southern Piedmont. The range turns northeast, bearing nearer the coast of the Middle Atlantic and New England states. Different parts of the Appalachians have their own labels. Tennessee has its Great Smokies and Cumberlands, which extend into eastern Kentucky and southwestern Virginia. The Alleghenies take over in Virginia and West Virginia, reaching up into Pennsylvania to southern New York and west over to eastern Ohio. The distinctive Blue Ridge Mountains lie east of the Alleghenies and extend from south-central Pennsylvania down to Georgia and Alabama. North into New York and New England are the Catskills, the Berkshires (in Connecticut and New York), the Green Mountains (Vermont), New Hampshire's White Mountains, and the rest of the range on beyond Maine to Quebec's Gaspe Peninsula. New York's tall Adirondacks are a southern extension of a Canadian system.

The high points on these variegated and jumbled mountain systems are not exceedingly lofty—5,000 and 6,000 feet or so. But many of the individual peaks are quite impressive because they rise as mountain structures from low valleys. New Hampshire's White Mountains have this kind of grandeur, with a dramatic upward sweep that belies their moderate altitudes. Those who are familiar with the Appalachian Mountains believe the chain was once possibly as tall or taller than the Alps and the Rockies and has been worn down by time and ice-age glaciers. Speculations about their former height seem reasonable, in light of the knowledge that these mountains are among the world's oldest. Their age is put at one-billion, one-million years, or 1,100-million years. Nothing and nobody would stand very tall after a life span like that.

The three southernmost states of the eastern region, Alabama, Georgia and Florida, are outside of the

New Jersey: 3rd State: December 18, 1787—Capital: Trenton   State Motto: *Liberty and Prosperity*

State Bird: Eastern Goldfinch   State Flower: Violet   State Tree: Red Oak

The William Trent House, Trenton   Scottish-born William Trent arrived in the area named "The Falls" in 1690. By 1719 he had developed a prosperous village and renamed it Trent Town. General George Washington and his soldiers entered Trenton on December 25, 1776, after crossing the icy waters of the Delaware River, defeating the Hessian mercenaries. New Jersey is cloaked in American Revolutionary and Civil War history. New Jersey is a highly industrialized state and densely populated. Chemical production leads the state's economy, while tourism, the insurance industry, research and development, and agriculture, which includes dairy farms and the production of cranberries, blueberries, peaches and apples, are economic contributors. Even though densely populated, there are abundant recreation sites, including National Park Service sites: Morristown, Edison, and the Delaware Water Gap; and the wilderness area's of Mettler's Woods and Island Beach offer nature investigation. There is a sparkling Atlantic seacoast well worth investigating. *Photo by Robert D. Shangle*

New Mexico: 47th State: January 6, 1912—Capital: Santa Fe   State Motto: *It Grows as it Goes*
State Bird: Roadrunner   State Flower: Yucca Flower   State Song: "O, Fair New Mexico"   State Tree: Piñon (Nut Pine)

White Sands National Monument, near Alamogordo   "At the northern end of the Chihauhaun Desert lies a mountain ringed valley called the Tularosa Basin. Rising from the heart of this basin is one of the world's great natural wonders—the glistening white sands of New Mexico." *(www.nps.gov)* High in altitude and dry in climate, New Mexico is diverse in terrain: the western third is a high plateau, the central third is home to the Rocky Mountains; the eastern third is part of the Great Plains. The Native American influence is dominant in the state's cultural history with such tribes as Pueblo, Utes, Navajo, Apache, Hopi, and Zuni. Investigating the national and state parks reveals the impact of the various tribes as they lived throughout the state. Cities such as Santa Fe, Albuquerque, Taos, Las Cruces, Roswell, Carlsbad, Hobbs, Clovis, and Gallup are harbors of interest intrinsic to New Mexico's culture and history. *Photo by Shangle Photographics*

Appalachians' domain, except for the northern hills of the first two. Florida may indeed be the flattest big piece of ground in the whole hemisphere, because most of it is at sea level and the highest of its few hills is 345 feet. But the Florida peninsula is really a separate piece of business from the land it is connected with. Once covered by the seas, it is still in close communion with oceanic waters. Its southern reach, from Lake Okeechobee on down, is wet and swampy except for a narrow limestone shoreline ridge. Water congregates all over the beautiful north of Florida, too, but there the lakes have a beginning and an end, and the ground is solid enough and fertile enough for a flourishing agriculture. Even though Florida calls itself "The Sunshine State," it receives a great deal of rain to replenish its immense underground limestone reservoirs, those watery places vital to the good health of its river, marshes and swamps, such as the Everglades.

One of the truly beautiful mountain groupings in the Appalachian system is the Great Smokies of Tennessee and North Carolina. These densely packed east-west ridges are an exception to the general north-south Appalachian profile. Their other worldly beauty is preserved in the Great Smoky Mountains National Park. Sugarlands Cove, one of the sheltered valleys in the park, and Greenbriar Cove north of it, are exceptionally well upholstered with stands of the world's finest hardwood trees. These and other sheltered mountain valleys, with their fertile soils resulting from the mountains' slow attrition, become a wildflower haven in the springtime. Both the flowers and the trees are remarkable in their variety.

One apparent anomaly of the southern Appalachians is the occurrence, here and there, of a grassy meadow in an ocean of dense forest. Usually found in the saddle between ridges, these openings, or balds, can be found from Georgia to Virginia. The early mountain settlers in the Blue Ridge valleys used them for pasture lands. This complex relationship with the mountains, involving the use of valley coves and summit grasslands in their daily activities, turned the settlers into mountain people. To make use of the two separated areas effectively, they had to explore the forested slopes and get to know the woods and the creatures that lived there. They learned to be self-sufficient in a way that is now unheard of, making everything they used from dwellings, to food and clothing, and tools and utensils. In the mountains of Tennessee and north Georgia, families and small communities still live a kind of pioneer life, cut off by choice from outside influence. Even speech patterns still show a shading of their Elizabethan forebears.

It comes as a shock to find out that the world's greatest concentration of deciduous broadleaf trees are in the forests of the Appalachians and the mountain borderlands. Add to that the conifers of the northern and southern mountains. The southern pines begin with a dense New Jersey forest belt that keeps going all the way to the piney woods of Georgia and northern Florida, then west to the Mississippi Delta country.

At least one hardwood tree common to Appalachia has a reputation that extends far beyond the eastern United States and indeed the Western Hemisphere. That tree is the sugar maple. It is found in abundance all over the range, from Georgia to Quebec. Vermont, of course, has sugar maples in great numbers, and the name Vermont has become almost inseparable from the idea of maple syrup. The varied Appalachian forests are put to a variety of uses other than making maple syrup and sugar. White and yellow pines from the north and south make strong building lumber. Some of the most beautiful and rugged woods—maple, black walnut and cherry— are fashioned into enduring furniture, from cabinets to gunstocks. White oak makes casks, charred on the inside, for holding distilled product important to the Tennessee economy. The nut trees, as the variety of forest

New York: 11th State: July 26, 1788—Capital: Albany State Motto: *Ever Upward*
State Bird: Bluebird   State Flower: Rose   State Song: "I Love New York"   State Tree: Sugar Maple

The American Falls at Niagara Falls Calculations indicate that 75,000 gallons of water flow over the 180-foot Falls each second, spread across the 1,075-foot width. This is just one of several locations in the immediate Niagara area that provides beauty and interest, both current and historical, as is true with the entire state. There is the Hudson Valley with the U. S. Military Academy, and Harriman State Park, and historical Newburgh; the ever popular Catskill Mountains, the Thousand Island area, the Finger Lakes, land of the Mohawk River, and the Adirondack Mountains. The state's boundaries are two of the Great Lakes: Erie on the west and Ontario on the north, plus the huge St. Lawrence River; Canada is on the upper north and Lake Champlain, Vermont, Massachusetts, and Connecticut border the eastern state line. Pennsylvania and New Jersey are on the south. New York's economic strength is like a kaleidoscope of color: ever changing and constantly there. *Photo by James Blank*

wildlife attests, do a good job of providing for the needs of other species besides the human one.

Many lines of poetry, countless essays, paintings and photographs have born witness to the autumnal display of color in the Appalachians. Everybody knows it happens, but nobody knows what it is all about until he has seen the real thing at least once. Easterners may take it for granted to some degree, but they, too, get impatient for the broadleaf show to begin in the fall. The long range has a long season of leaf-turning. The brilliant reds and golds begin blazing forth in the crisp New England October, then a little later the hills of New York and Pennsylvania will take up the theme, in a fairyland kaleidoscope of soft shades and tints. Finally, the southland's mountains and hills will yield to autumn's palette, glowing in subtle hues that seem to arouse a deep emotional response in the onlooker.

New Englanders have a reputation for being tough and taciturn, with a dollop of ingenuity added to the mix. It is easy to see how all that developed. The early Pilgrims found the land rocky and infertile and the winter ferocious. They and those who came after them developed endurance to withstand the climate, and acquired business acumen to make it in a region where farming on a commercial scale was not feasible. The taciturnity probably developed from a necessity to put all their energy into doing instead of talking. The New Englander's sense of self-reliance is an American legend. He got that way by using self-taught skills to prepare himself to make a living, whether by fishing the stormy, marine-rich North Atlantic or by being involved in some kind of manufacturing. Since the beginning fishing has been of prime importance in New England, where the jagged coastline offers numberless natural harbors. The early settler quickly found great resources in the dense and varied forests of the region's mountains, and handy transportation in the rivers rushing out of those mountains.

North Carolina: 12th State: November 21, 1789—**Capital: Raleigh**   State Motto: *To Be, rather than To Seem*
State Bird: Cardinal   State Flower: Flowering Dogwood   State Song: "The Old North State"   State Tree: Pine

Statue of Marquis de LaFayette, Fayetteville   The city of Fayetteville was officially established in 1778, but roots go back to the Highland Scots of Argyllshire who first settled in 1736. Fayetteville was named in 1783 to honor Marquis de LaFayette, relinquishing the previous name of "Upper and Lower Campbellton." Located on the Cape Fear River gave the town importance as a trade center. In 1849 the first and longest of the plank roads was built out from Fayetteville, providing improved transportation links to other parts of the state. Rugged and forested mountains cover well-over a third of North Carolina. Multiple waterfalls, lakes and rivers offer recreation opportunities only limited by personal inactivity. The mountain ranges include the Appalachian, Blue Ridge and Great Smoky mountains. North Carolina leads in tobacco production and sweet potatoes as well as a national leader in hogs and turkeys, Christmas trees, pickling cucumbers, lima beans and turnip greens. Today, military presence is most evident in North Carolina: Fort Bragg, Pope Air Force Base, and Camp Lejeune. *Photo by Robert D. Shangle*

North Dakota: 39th State: November 2, 1889—Bismarck   State Motto: *Liberty and Union, Now and Forever, One and Inseparable*

State Bird: Western Meadowlark   State Flower: Wild Prairie Rose   State Song: "North Dakota Hymn"   State Tree: American Elm

The Little Missouri River in the Theodore Roosevelt National Park, North Unit   Referred to as the badlands, these irregular erosional plateaus and gouged gullies appear to be a spring garden. Wind, water and sand attack the earth carving these unusual land formations. Theodore Roosevelt, the 26th-President of the United States, loved this area and lived here for a period of time. North Dakota's history is framed by the strong influence of the Native American culture: Mandan, Arikara, Hidatsa, Cheyenne, Cree, Sioux, Blackfeet, Crow, and Ojibwa (Chippewa). The French Canadians penetrated the area by the mid-1700s, establishing ownership of much of the land in mid-America by the French. Western North Dakota was purchased by the United States through the Louisiana Purchase in 1803, and the eastern portion was obtained from Great Britain in 1818 when the International Boundary Line was established at the 49th parallel. Cattle and cattle products lead the state's economy followed by agricultural products with such items as wheat, barley, sugar beets, oats, soybeans, and sunflowers. *Photo by Shangle Photographics*

Ever since, they have made use of these resources in connection with their seaports to build up great industries.

Many things are changing in New England, just as in the rest of the country these days. The cities, especially, are doing what cities all across the continent have been doing ever since the dream of motorized mobility became a reality. They are changing their faces in ways that reflect a style of life less identified with the place. Boston, New Haven, Hartford and such march to the beat that moves today's world; but nothing can destroy the ambience of these oldest of American cities. And, of course, most of New England is not cities. Some of the real beauty of the area is to be found in the countryside: small-scale communities hold onto an appearance and style of life more characteristic of the past than the present. They fit into the hilly interior or on their rocky coastal sites like a natural part of the landscape. The weathered coastal villages have no counterpart over the whole spread of the country.

As if to compensate for some of the harsher aspects of weather that often visit this part of the country, nature has ornamented inland New England with some of the Appalachians' most gorgeous mountain ranges. The White Mountains of Maine and New Hampshire are among the most impressive heights in the East. Their Presidential Range includes Mt. Washington's 6,288-foot pinnacle, highest in the Northeast. The elevation, the latitude, and the savage North Atlantic Ocean have made the tall peak a mountain of storms. It is a great tourist draw in the summer (and very pleasant at that time of year), but snows and high winds keep it closed to visitors from fall through late spring. The glamorous Whites are now, over much of their extent, protected as a national forest, so that logging activities are controlled. The fact of their preservation, after being long in the hands of private lumber companies, indicates a growing concern on the side of the environment in a part of the country

Marblehead Lighthouse, Lake Erie This 65-foot structure, the oldest active lighthouse on the Great Lakes, was built in 1821 and has acted as a navigational guide since 1822. Whale-oil lamps were the first lights, followed by kerosene lamps in 1858. Electricity was introduced in 1923 and the light was automated in 1958. Civilian lighthouse keepers were replaced by the United States Coast Guard in 1946. Though the Coast Guard still maintains the lighthouse beacon, the Ohio Dept. of Natural Resources has maintained the property since 1972 and took ownership of the light tower in 1998. The enactment of the Northwest Territory in 1787 opened the land to settlers who quickly emigrated to the Ohio Territory. They found rich farmland, abundant amounts of oil, natural gas, coal, iron ore, and great hardwood forests. Diversification was the watchword in Ohio, and still is today, with its bounty of agricultural, manufacturing and service products. The land is smooth in the north away from Lake Erie, extending to a more rolling-hills terrain moving south. *Photo by Shangle Photographics*

that has many times set an example for the rest of the nation in its emphasis on the values that are important.

The coastal East has a long reach, from north to south and east toward Europe. The New England shore leans so far out into the North Atlantic that on a map it seems to be trying to connect up with the Old World again. The New England "tilt" is one of the geographical distinctions of the northeast coast. The marvelously complicated coastal strip of Maine displays a dazzling array of land and sea interrelationships. This "drowned" shore was created many millennia ago when Ice Age glaciers humbled coastal mountain ranges under their tremendous weight, pushing them deeper into the earth. So later on when the glaciers retreated, the valleys became inlets and fjords and the peaks became islands surrounded by crooked arms of the sea. Now some of these islands are numbered among our most prized and unspoiled offshore wildlife sanctuaries. Although the worst winter poundings are usually reserved for the North Atlantic provinces of Canada, the state of Maine gets its share of icy oceanic savagery. But the punishing sea is a nourisher too, enriching the seascape with a kind of beauty only possible as the gentler face of a sometimes fierce land-sea confrontation.

To a person only vaguely familiar with the term, "Down East" means anywhere in New England. But the true Yankee narrows the expression to its historical sense, meaning the coast of Maine. Coastal shipping was once said to be headed Down East when traveling north, downwind, along the eastward-turning coast of Maine. It is often a foggy coastline, especially along the part farthest Down East. The fog, which occurs at any season, is caused when two competing ocean streams, the cold Labrador current and the warm Gulf Stream, mix it up somewhere offshore. At such times the dense woodlands that grow on offshore islands become even more wild and mysterious. The rocky coastal strip seems to have a "just-made" look anyway, enhanced by fog-shrouded mystery. Mt. Desert Island, part of the offshore conglomeration, is a king-size example of these enchanted kingdoms, twelve by sixteen miles big. It has thick forests, many lakes, and a range of variety in its plant and bird life that intrigues naturalists year-round.

Its location on one of the major bird migration routes doesn't hurt either, as John James Audubon discovered to his delight. In addition it has also attracted the migratory wealthy of East Coast society, who originally founded the community of Bar Harbor for the purpose of studying their own kind. Now the town is more tourist than exclusive, its reincarnation abetted by the establishment of Acadia National Park on a fifth of the island and a part of the adjacent mainland.

The lower New England coastal profile sticks a very long nose into the Atlantic at Cape Cod. It actually looks more like an arm, bent at the elbow, and making a fist. Whatever shape it is in, Cape Cod gives Massachusetts a 65-mile foot in the ocean. The Cape's long outer beach, from the arm's bend to land's end at Race point, is still about as unspoiled as it was when the glaciers and the ocean put it together, even with the summer multitudes that swarm onto it. Its glittery waters, bright sands, and high-rise dunes are protected in the Cape Cod National Seashore. The upper part of the arm is, the east-west portion, with two distinct shores: Cape Cod Bay is on the western side of the land mass and the Atlantic Ocean laps onto the eastern shore. The northern "fist" is where Provincetown claims primary domain. Nantucket Sound pushes up to the southern edge of the arm of land, where many Bostonians and New Yorkers have established summer homes. The Cape's southern beach is further enhanced as a vacation mecca by the presence in Nantucket Sound with the islands of Martha's Vineyard and Nantucket. These two beautiful pieces of glacial litter have preserved their quiet ways and their old-time charms

Oklahoma: 46th State: November 16, 1907—Capital: Oklahoma City State Motto: *Labor conquers all Things*
State Bird: Scissor-Tailed Flycatcher   State Flower: Mistletoe   State Song: "Oklahoma"   State Tree: Redbud

Oklahoma City Located near the center of the state, Oklahoma City is the center of state government and many state activities. Oklahoma is a center of oil production and a leader in the nation for natural gas production. Agriculture is by far one of the most important commodities in Oklahoma, claiming a leadership position in the production of wheat, pecans, peanuts and peaches. Cattle ranching and calf production is big business too. And that leads to big-time rodeo activities. With a history of being a crossroads of cattle trails out of Texas heading to the railroads in Kansas, there were plenty of cowboys, those caretakers of cattle who rode their horse from dawn to dusk and sometimes all night, if needed. These cowboys liked to display their "skills" on their pony and how they could work the cattle. Those "skills" developed into a rodeo: a gathering together of strong, athletic folks who showed what a cowboy could do. Rodeos are a real part of Oklahoma, throughout the entire state. West Oklahoma is high, dry plains; the east is rolling hills; through the center is the Arkansas River Basin in the north, and the Red River Plains are in the south. *Photo by Robert D. Shangle*

Crater Lake in Crater Lake National Park, southern Cascade Mountains   The sapphire-blue waters of Crater Lake reach a depth of 1,932 feet, making it the deepest lake in North America. A severe volcanic eruption some 7,700-years ago caused the top portion of Mt. Mazama to collapse, creating a vast caldera that gradually filled with water. A 33-mile road around the lake allows a visitor to enjoy a more personal involvement with the lake area. Oregon is a land of diversity. Mountains prevail in the western third of the state with a large productive valley in the midst; high desert takes over through a great portion of middle Oregon to the California border on the south; from mid-central to the northeast section,high mountains control the terrain, many reaching beyond 10,000 feet in height. The Pacific Ocean coastline provides a unique beauty to the entire length of the state's western boundary. Volcanic activity has created many natural wonders of prime interest. *Photo by James Blank*

in the face of increasing attention from the vacation crowds of the Eastern Seaboard. Famed Narragansett Bay, carving up little Rhode Island to the west, has Providence at its head and Newport down by the ocean end, both towns of considerable lustre in a historical and social context.

Long Island Sound comes up next, like a watery underline closing off the New England profile. The Sound introduces the country's biggest city to the Atlantic Ocean, and indeed, New Yorkers regard it as their very own sea. Connecticut, comprising the Sound's north shore, also has some claim to it. Long Island itself is effectively part of New York City, its western end a distinctive cityscape and the rest of it a suburb, albeit an attractive one.

The intricate waterfront of New York City's vast harbor is all business, including the Bronx, Manhattan and Staten Island, although once in awhile an isolated patch of open land, almost rural, makes a bright surprise appearance in the midst of countless piers and warehouses, and wharf buildings and ships, and expressways. North Jersey pokes its intensely industrialized shoreline into this frenetic manufacturing and service complex, too. But other parts of this smallish coastal state dance to a different tune. The South Jersey shore, to cite a notorious example, is beach country with a vengeance, and because of its handy proximity to New York and Philadelphia, both heavily used and heavily publicized. Atlantic City used to be the destination of the summer social set from the big cities. Now of course the gambling casinos have refurbished its reputation as a place to be. And it doesn't hurt for it to have some of those white-sand beaches strung out for miles and miles and miles along South Jersey's island ramparts. The beaches are still the number one draw in the state, outdistancing even oil refineries and gambling as revenue producers.

The Middle Atlantic coast is sidetracked in a large fashion in the New Jersey-Delaware-Maryland-Virginia vicinity by those two estuaries, Chesapeake Bay and Delaware Bay. The bigger by far is the Chesapeake, carving up Maryland good and proper. It reaches up into that state for 200 miles. The Bay's convoluted shoreline pinches in to four miles near its head and widens to forty elsewhere. The Eastern Shore—always referred to in capital letters—is still relatively unpopulated. Its quiet backwaters are idyllic retreats for man, beast, and fish. The Chesapeake's fishy reputation is no fluke, because it is home to more than 400 species of marine life. Fortunate Easterners who live near enough to its shores grow content on the Bay's provender.

North Carolina's Outer Banks are a long string of barrier islands that frame her coastline. Some of them are protected by inclusion in the seventy-mile long Cape Hatteras National Seashore. The Cape itself guards the coast with its tall lighthouse, warning shipping away from the shallows around it. The islands follow the coastline as it swings southwest; they have become seaside resorts after long isolation from the mainland. The Banks and the shore proper of both North and South Carolina are still places that live in a time warp, with the past intertwined with the present. Tales of shipwrecks and pirate hideaways are familiar ingredients in the lives of the Banks residents. The islands have the best of two present-day worlds—ocean surf on one side and the quiet waters of a sound on the other.

The coast's outrigger islands occur in a more-or-less continuous chain all the way from New Jersey to Florida and into the Gulf of Mexico. The sometimes-narrow passage between island and mainland is on occasion the route of the elusive and eccentric Intracoastal (or Inland) Waterway that wanders along rivers, creeks, bays, estuaries, canals, and swamps, staying just back of the shoreline except when occasionally forced into open

Pennsylvania: 2nd State: December 12, 1787—Capital: Harrisburg State Motto: *Virtue, Liberty and Independence*

State Bird: Ruffed Grouse   State Flower: Mountain Laurel   State Song: "Pennsylvania"   State Tree: Hemlock

Gen. George Washington's Headquarters, Valley Forge National Historical Park   Arriving on December 19, 1777, it was from this house owned by Issac Potts that Gen. Washington and his staff conducted the daily routine of the army while wintering his troops. Records indicate that when Gen. Washington occupied the house, he paid his landlord one-hundred pounds Pennsylvania hard-coin currency as rent money for a six-month period. The General occupied the house until June 19, 1778. The state's natural beauty is partly a function of the Blue and Allegheny mountains that sweep diagonally across it, ridge after ridge. Its population centers, large and small, have maintained their historical integrity. History saturates every inch of the state: the American Revolution, the Civil War, and economic evolutions that have effected the state's development as a center of manufacturing. *Photo by Robert D. Shangle*

water. The famed "Golden Isles" of Georgia—Cumberland, St. Simons and Sapelo among them—form an honor guard for the Waterway. Georgia's offshore treasures, or some of them at least, are surprising examples of the gorgeous coastal wilderness still in existence on the southeastern shoreline. Still farther south, the elusive Florida coast hides behind offshore island beaches nearly all of the 350 miles or more to the tip of the peninsula. A few of these sand spits have been promoted to celebrity status far beyond what would surely be expected of a sea-girt piece of coral rock or a limestone ridge covered by an overcoat of white sand. A few of these that come quickly to mind are Daytona Beach, Cape Canaveral and Miami Beach.

Broadly speaking, the various wonders of the nation's eastern shores do not end with the Everglades National Park on the point of the Florida Peninsula. The Florida Keys dribble on for another hundred miles. These coral rocks curve in a southwest arc toward the Gulf. The clear, shallow waters of the coral reef bordering the Keys are ablaze with color from the living coral and from the gaudy marine life that frequents the coral ridges and recesses. The water around the Keys is warm, but beaches are scanty. Off big Key Largo the "beach" is under water in Pennekamp State Park, where skin divers may go exploring.

There is still much more to the Florida coastal story, to be sure. The longer part of the state's shoreline is on the Gulf side, curving north and west up along the Panhandle to Pensacola. Except in the TampA Bay vicinity, the west side is thinly populated. Its lavish natural gifts include a great abundance of offshore islands and rich estuarine waters where wildlife, from alligators to egrets, come in to its own. If the country's eastern shoreline must end somewhere, probably Florida's Gulf side with its miles and miles of pristine coast puts a fitting cap on it all.

Rhode Island: 13th State: May 29, 1790—Capital: Providence   State Motto: *Hope*

State Bird: Rhode Island Red   State Flower: Violet   State Song: "Rhode Island"   State Tree: Red Maple

The Gilbert Stuart Birthplace near Saunderstown   America's Master Painter, Gilbert Stuart's artworks, which includes several paintings of George Washington, are seen in museums and galleries around the world. Here his father began the first waterpowered tobacco snuff mill in the colonies. Stuart was born on December 3, 1755, long after the Rhode Island colony was established. Roger Williams established the first permanent settlement at Providence in 1635. This beautiful little state is nestled between Connecticut on the west and Massachusetts on the north and east. The Atlantic Ocean pushes up from the south, penetrating inland for 28 miles by way of the Narraganset Bay. East to west, Rhode Island is a maximun of 37-miles wide and 48-miles long. Its shoreline is approximately 385 miles, traversing the entire water frontage, which includes all the bays and waterways of southern Rhode Island. *Photo by Robert D. Shangle*

South Carolina: 8th State: May 23, 1788—Capital: Columbia   State Motto: *While I Breathe, I Hope*

State Bird: Carolina Wren   State Flower: Carolina Jessamine   State Song: "Carolina"   State Tree: Palmetto

The Long Bridge at Magnolia Plantation and its Gardens in Charleston   This plantation was a wedding gift from Steven Fox to Thomas Drayton, Jr. and his daughter, Ann, in the latter part of the 1600s. Ownership is maintained by Drayton ancestry today. John Grimke Drayton, who brought the first azalea and camellia plants to America, created the oldest public attraction in America. South Carolina is a land of resilience having experienced the ravages of the American Revolution, the scars of the Civil War and devastation of weather. The Atlantic Ocean is the southeast border, where the Grand Strand and multiple islands create an area of adventure. The Upland Region of the northwest is heavily forested and brimming with lakes and waterfalls within the Blue Ridge Mountains. The Savannah River forms a natural boundary with Georgia to the south. The Catawba, Great Pee Dee, Broad, and Savannah rivers open recreational activity unexcelled. *Photo by James Blank*

President George Bush, Inaugural Address, Continued from page 17

But the stakes for America are never small. If our country does not lead the cause of freedom, it will not be led. If we do not turn the hearts of children toward knowledge and character, we will lose their gifts and undermine their idealism. If we permit our economy to drift and decline, the vulnerable will suffer most.

We must live up to the calling we share. Civility is not a tactic or a sentiment. It is the determined choice of trust over cynicism, of community over chaos. And this commitment, if we keep it, is a way to shared accomplishment.

America, at its best, is also courageous.

Our national courage has been clear in times of depression and war, when defending common dangers defined our common good. Now we must choose if the example of our fathers and mothers will inspire us or condemn us. We must show courage in a time of blessing by confronting problems instead of passing them on to future generations.

Together, we will reclaim America's schools, before ignorance and apathy claim more young lives.

We will reform Social Security and Medicare, sparing our children from struggles we have the power to prevent. And we will reduce taxes, to recover the momentum of our economy and reward the effort and enterprise of working Americans.

We will build our defenses beyond challenge, lest weakness invite challenge.

We will confront weapons of mass destruction, so that a new century is spared new horrors.

The enemies of liberty and our country should make no mistake. America remains engaged in the world by

South Dakota: 40th State: November 2, 1889—Capital: Pierre   State Motto: *Under God the People Rule*

State Bird: Ring-necked Pheasant   State Flower: Pasqueflower   State Song: "Hail South Dakota"   State Tree: Black Hills Spruce

Mount Rushmore National Memorial near Keystone   "Mount Rushmore memorializes the birth, growth, preservation and development of the United States of America. Between 1927 and 1941, Gutzon Borglum and 400 workers sculpted the 60-foot busts of Presidents George Washington, Thomas Jefferson, Theodore Roosevelt, and Abraham Lincoln to represent the first 150 years of American history." *(www.nps.gov)* When the United States bought the land known as the Louisiana Purchase from France in 1803, South Dakota became U. S. Property. The exploration by Lewis and Clark in 1804-1806 created the first written record about the area and the expedition opened the land to the inquiring settler. The Great Sioux Nation encompassed the Dakota land. Such names as Crazy Horse and Sitting Bull add to the burgeoning history that clings to South Dakota. The vast prairie land and rolling hills are broken only by the Black Hills in the southwest corner of the state. There is plenty of cowboy and Indian history here; tremendous stories about probing setters, Native American, and the U. S. Cavalry; military forts and sod houses. *Photo by James Blank*

history and by choice, shaping a balance of power that favors freedom. We will defend our allies and our interests. We will show purpose without arrogance. We will meet aggression and bad faith with resolve and strength. And to all nations, we will speak for the values that gave our nation birth.

America, at its best, is compassionate. In the quiet of American conscience, we know that deep, persistent poverty is unworthy of our nation's promise.

And whatever our views of its cause, we can agree that children at risk are not at fault. Abandonment and abuse are not acts of God, they are failures of love.

And the proliferation of prisons, however necessary, is no substitute for hope and order in our souls.

Where there is suffering, there is duty. Americans in need are not strangers, they are citizens, not problems, but priorities. And all of us are diminished when any are hopeless.

Government has great responsibilities for public safety and public health, for civil rights and common schools. Yet compassion is the work of a nation, not just a government.

And some needs and hurts are so deep they will only respond to a mentor's touch or a pastor's prayer. Church and charity, synagogue and mosque lend our communities their humanity, and they will have an honored place in our plans and in our laws.

Many in our country do not know the pain of poverty, but we can listen to those who do.

And I can pledge our nation to a goal: When we see that wounded traveler on the road to Jericho, we will not pass to the other side.

Continued on next page

America, at its best, is a place where personal responsibility is valued and expected.

Encouraging responsibility is not a search for scapegoats, it is a call to conscience. And though it requires sacrifice, it brings a deeper fulfillment. We find the fullness of life not only in options, but in commitments. And we find that children and community are the commitments that set us free.

Our public interest depends on private character, on civic duty and family bonds and basic fairness, on uncounted, unhonored acts of decency which give direction to our freedom.

Sometimes in life we are called to do great things. But as a saint of our times has said, every day we are called to do small things with great love. The most important tasks of a democracy are done by everyone.

I will live and lead by these principles: to advance my convictions with civility, to pursue the public interest with courage, to speak for greater justice and compassion, to call for responsibility and try to live it as well.

In all these ways, I will bring the values of our history to the care of our times.

What you do is as important as anything government does. I ask you to seek a common good beyond your comfort; to defend needed reforms against easy attacks; to serve your nation, beginning with your neighbor. I ask you to be citizens; citizens, not spectators; citizens, not subjects; responsible citizens, building communities of service and a nation of character.

Americans are generous and strong and decent, not because we believe in ourselves, but because we hold beliefs beyond our selves. When this spirit of citizenship is missing, no government program can replace it. When this spirit is present, no wrong can stand against it.

After the Declaration of Independence was signed, Virginia statesman John Page wrote to Thomas Jefferson:

Continued on next page

Tennessee: 16th State: June 1, 1796—Capital: Nashville State Motto: *Agriculture and Commerce*
State Bird: Mockingbird   State Flower: Iris   State Song: "The Tennessee Waltz"   State Tree: Tulip Poplar

Belle Meade Plantation, Nashville Nineteenth-century heritage is protected at the Belle Meade, referred to as the "Queen of Tennessee Plantations." Surviving the Civil War was a feat of accomplishment for the old house, as evidence of bullets hitting the stone columns is still displayed. History plays a key role in Tennessee's success. Think of Tennessee and country music comes to mind, a strong economic contributor to Tennessee's success. Agriculture is the lead indicator of Tennessee achievement. Nearly half of the state's land is in farms. "Tennessee is the nation's leading manufacturer of hardwood flooring, log homes, and pencils" *(Tennessee Blue Book)* and is a national leader in hardwood lumber. Beef cattle, horse farms, tobacco and nursery stock add to the mix of agricultural success, along with soybeans, wheat, corn, cotton, and sorghum. *Photo by Shangle Photographics*

"We know the race is not to the swift nor the battle to the strong. Do you not think an angel rides in the whirlwind and directs this storm?"

Much time has passed since Jefferson arrived for his inauguration. The years and changes accumulate. But the themes of this day he would know: our nation's grand story of courage and its simple dream of dignity.

We are not this story's author, who fills time and eternity with his purpose. Yet his purpose is achieved in our duty, and our duty is fulfilled in service to one another.

Never tiring, never yielding, never finishing, we renew that purpose today, to make our country more just and generous, to affirm the dignity of our lives and every life.

This work continues. This story goes on. And an angel still rides in the whirlwind and directs this storm.

God bless you all, and God bless America.

President George W. Bush
43rd President of the United States
Inaugural Address
January 20, 2001

Texas: 28th State: December 29, 1845—Capital: Austin State Motto: *Friendship*

State Bird: Mockingbird   State Flower: Bluebonnet   State Song: "Texas, Our Texas"   State Tree: Pecan

The Alamo, San Antonio First known as Mission San Antonio de Valero, founded in 1718 by Franciscan missionaries, the mission was secularized in 1793 and then used as a military post, occupied by troops from the area near El Alamo in Mexico in 1803, serving as a parish church. The struggle for independence ensued over the next few years, culminating in a battle that involved the old mission, known by then as the Alamo. Beginning March 6, 1836, the defending forces, which included Jim Bowie, Davey Crockett, and William Travis, lost their lives battling General Santa Anna and his troops. Because of its size, 266,807-square miles, climate and terrain vary in Texas: west Texas is very dry; north and west-central Texas is moderate; east-central has abundant rain; and east Texas can have too much rain. The state of New Mexico borders on the west, with Oklahoma to the north. Arkansas and Louisiana are to the east. Mexico is to the south, with the Rio Grande separating the two countries. *Photo by Shangle Photographics*

Delicate Arch, Arches National Park near Moab   "Arches National Park preserves over two thousand natural sandstone arches, including the world-famous Delicate Arch, in addition to a variety of unique geological resources and formations. In some areas, faulting has exposed millions of years of geologic history. The extraordinary features of the park, including balanced rocks, fins and pinnacles, are highlighted by a striking environment of contrasting colors, landforms and textures." *www.nps.gov)* Utah is blessed with outstanding natural wonders protected by other National Parks: Bryce Canyon, Capitol Reef, Canyonlands and Zion. National Monuments include Cedar Breaks, Dinosaur, and Grand Staircase. National Recreation Areas include Flaming Gorge and Glen Canyon. Utah is home to the world's fourth-largest terminal (no outlet) lake in the world, the Great Salt Lake, three to five times saltier than the ocean. *Photo by Virginia Swartzendruber*

Concord Hymn
(The shot heard round the world)

By Ralph Waldo Emerson
The Concord Hymn was written to commemorate the
battle for independence at Concord, Massachusetts, on April 19, 1775, at the North Bridge.
It was first sung July 4, 1837, at the completion of the battle monument.

Verse I

By the rude bridge that arched the flood
    Their flag to April's breeze unfurled,
Here once the embattled farmers stood
    And fired the shot heard round the world.

Verse II

The foe long since in silence slept;
    Alike the conqueror silent sleeps;
And Time the ruined bridge has swept
    Down the dark stream which seaward creeps.

Verse III

On this green bank, by this soft stream,
    We set today a votive stone;
That memory may their deed redeem,
    When, like our sires, our sons are gone.

Verse IV

Spirit, that made those heroes dare
    To die, and leave their children free,
Bid Time and Nature gently spare
    The shaft we raise to them and thee.

The village of Topsham   Vermont is extremely sensitive to "Nature's Special Season," Autumn, and to the beautiful foliage colors. Throughout central Vermont, the fall colors begin their appearance the last tens days of September, carrying through to mid-October. All of Vermont is a verdant delight, capturing its ever presence in the Green Mountains that span the state north and south. Huge Lake Champlain borders two-thirds of Vermont's western border along with New York in the southwest. Quebec, Canada, is on the north, the state of New Hampshire is on the east, separated by the beautiful Connecticut River. For winter snowfall Vermont is where you'll find it, providing endless skiing opportunities for the cross-country or downhill skier. Vermont is known for its maple sugar, exceeded by dairy products, cattle, hay, and apple production. *Photo by James Blank*

Words of Wisdom by Great Americans

"Today, we need a nation of Minutemen, citizens who are not only prepared to take arms, but citizens who regard the preservation of freedom as the basic purpose of their daily life and who are willing to consciously work and sacrifice for that freedom."—*John F. Kennedy*

"He who has done his duty honestly, and according to his best skill and judgement, stands acquitted before God and man."—*Thomas Jefferson*

"They that can give up essential liberty to purchase a little temporary safety, deserve neither liberty or safety."—*Benjamin Franklin*

"If to be venerated for benevolence, if to be admired for talents, if to be esteemed for patriotism, if to be beloved for philanthropy can gratify the human mind, you must have the pleasing consolation to know that you have not lived in vain."—*George Washington*

"The strength of the Constitution lies in the will of the people to defend it."—*Thomas Edison*

Words of Wisdom by Great Americans

"If a Nation expects to be ignorant and free in a state of civilization, it expects what never was and never will be…. If we are to guard against ignorance and remain free, it is the responsibility of every American to be informed."—*Thomas Jefferson*

"Freedom from fear and injustice and oppression will be ours only in the measure that men who value such freedom are ready to sustain its possession…to defend it against every thrust from within and without."—*Dwight David Eisenhower*

"To act coolly, intelligently and prudently in perilous circumstances is the test of a man and also a nation."—*Adlai Stevenson*

"Far better it is to dare mighty things, to win glorious triumphs, even though checkered by failure, than to take rank with those poor spirits who neither enjoy much nor suffer much, because they live in the gray twilight that knows not victory nor defeat."—*Theodore Roosevelt*

"The said Constitution shall never be construed to authorize Congress to prevent the people of the United States who are peaceable citizens from keeping their own arms."—*Samuel Adams*

Virginia: 10th State: June 25, 1788—Capital: Richmond   State Motto: *Thus Always to Tyrants*
State Bird: Cardinal   State Flower: Dogwood   State Song: "Carry Me Back to Old Virginia"   State Tree: Dogwood

The Governor's Palace, Williamsburg   This historic city was first settled in 1632 as Middle Plantation but renamed in 1699. It has been home to the College of William and Mary since 1693. Historic Williamsburg is by most accounts a reconstructed village that perpetuates early American history surrounding the American Revolution. Virginia *is history* : past and present. Jamestown was the first permanent English-speaking settlement in North America, founded in 1607. Virginia's sons played a crucial role in the American Revolution. There were more battles fought in Virginia during the Civil War than in any other state. Virginia is endowed with natural beauty such as found in the Appalachian Mountains, the Blue Ridge Mountains and Shenandoah National Park. The rivers and lakes, Chesapeake Bay, and the Atlantic Ocean are a realm unequaled by most standards. *Photo by James Blank*

Words of Wisdom by Great Americans

"We have staked the whole future of American civilization, not upon the power of government, far from it. We have staked the future…upon the capacity of each and all of us to govern ourselves, to sustain ourselves, according to the Ten Commandments of God."—*James Madison*

"The people of the United States are the rightful masters of both Congress and the courts, not to overthrow the Constitution, but to overthrow the men who pervert the Constitution."—*Abraham Lincoln*

"God grants liberty only to those who love it, and are always ready to guard and defend it."—*Daniel Webster*

"A decent and manly examination of the acts of Government should not only be tolerated, but encouraged."—*William Henry Harrison*

"Government is a trust, and the officers of the government are trustees; and both the trust and trustees are created for the benefit of the people."—*Henry Clay*

"Rebellion to tyrants is obedience to God."—*Thomas Jefferson*

Washington: 42nd State: November 11, 1889—Capital: Olympia State Motto: *Bye and Bye*

State Bird: Willow Goldfinch   State Flower: Coast Rhododendron   State Song: "Washington My Home"   State Tree: Western Hemlock

Mount St. Helens In March 1980, a small crater appeared near the summit of Mt. St. Helens after a minor volcanic eruption, the first activity since 1857. Through April and early May, small eruptions occurred. On the morning of May 18th, the north side of the mountain exploded, spewing debris with a power that was over 500-times greater than the bomb dropped on Hiroshima, Japan, during World War II. The heat and force of the blast destroyed 200-square-miles of forest, leaving behind massive downed trees that looked like match sticks. Today, flowers have taken hold and the ridges have green plants and trees again. Many wild animals have returned to their home. Mother Nature has created something new, just as she has been doing all throughout the beautiful state of Washington for eons. The Olympic Mountains on the western front along the Pacific Ocean is one of her creations, along with Puget Sound. The massive northern Cascade Mountains hold many natural wonders waiting to be explored, along with the Columbia Basin through the central portion of the state, and the highland of the northeast. The aerospace and forestry industries are leaders for the economy along with food products and agriculture. *Photo by Doug Lorain.*

West Virginia: 35th State: June 20, 1863—Capital: Charleston   State Motto: *Mountaineers are Always Free*

State Bird: Cardinal   State Flower: Rhododendron   State Song: "The West Virginia Hills"   State Tree: Sugar Maple

Babcock State Park, Fayette County   The Park "offers its guests 4,127 acres of serene, yet rugged beauty, a fast flowing trout stream in a boulder-strewn canyon and mountainous vistas to be viewed from several scenic overlooks. All of this variety is located adjacent to the New River Gorge National River and the heart of the white water rafting industry of West Virginia." *(www.babcocksp.com)* Even though there are many natural settings set aside as protected areas, West Virginia has abundant forest land, and lumber has long been an important hardwood resource. Other natural resources include bituminous coal, natural gas, stone, cement, salt and oil. Though available farm land is restricted, apples, peaches, hay, corn and tobacco are important to the state's economy. *Photo by Shangle Photographics*

Words of Wisdom by Great Americans

"No free man shall ever be de-barred the use of arms. The strongest reason for the people to retain their right to keep and bear arms is as a last resort to protect themselves against tyranny in government."—*Thomas Jefferson*

"Man will ultimately be governed by God or by tyrants."—*Benjamin Franklin*

"I would remind you; extremism in the defense of liberty is no vice…. And let me remind you also, moderation in the pursuit of justice is no virtue."—*Barry Goldwater*

"…arms…discourage and keep the invader in awe, and preserve order in the world as well as property. …Horrid mischief would ensue were (the law-abiding) derived the use of them."——*Thomas Paine*

"You have rights antecedent to all earthly governments; that cannot be repealed or restrained by human laws; rights derived from the Great Legislator of the Universe."—*John Adams*

"Government is not reason; it is not eloquence; it is force! Like fire, it is a dangerous servant and a fearful master."—*George Washington*

Wisconsin: 30th State: May 29, 1848—Capital: Madison State Motto: *Forward*

State Bird: Robin   State Flower: Wood Violet   State Song: "On Wisconsin"   State Tree: Sugar Maple

In southeast Wisconsin This handsome family farm in Walsworth County represents the dignity of rich farmland and nature's abundance afforded to Wisconsin. Eight out of ten farmers are dairy farmers and the state produces more cheese than the other forty-nine combined. Dairying is common to every part of the state. The elongated, softly contoured hillocks deposited by the glacier make great pastures and provide scenery for painters and photographers. The small lakes and streams and the cultivation of woodlots combine to create an idyllic atmosphere of settled prosperity. Natures wonders in Wisconsin include the Apostle Islands of Lake Superior, thousands of lakes strewn all over the state, river systems that have drain fields that extend north to Lake Superior, southeast to Lake Michigan, and south into the state of Illinois. The beautiful St. Croix River is nature's western boundary next to Minnesota. *Photo by Shangle Photographics*

Words of Wisdom by Great Americans

"Let every nation know, whether it wishes us well or ill, that we shall pay any price, bear any burden, meet any hardship, support any friend, oppose any foe, in order to assure the survival and the success of liberty."— *John F. Kennedy*

"I am only one, but I am one. I cannot do everything, but I can do something. What I can do, I should do and, with the help of God, I will do!"—*Everett Hale*

"The fundamental basis of this nation's law was given to Moses on the Mount. The fundamental basis of our Bill of Rights comes from the teachings we get from Exodus and St. Matthew, from Isaiah and St. Paul."—*Harry S. Truman*

"If ye love wealth better than liberty, the tranquillity of servitude better than the animating contest of freedom, go home from us in peace. We ask not your counsels or your arms. Crouch down and lick the hands which feed you. May your chains set lightly upon you, and may prosperity forget that ye were our countrymen."—*Samuel Adams*

"The time to guard against corruption and tyranny is before they shall have gotten hold of us. It is better to keep the wolf out of the fold than to trust to drawing his teeth and talons after he shall have entered."—*Thomas Jefferson*

Wyoming: 44th State: July 10, 1890—Capital: Cheyenne State Motto: *Equal Rights*

State Bird: Meadowlark   State Flower: Indian Paintbrush   State Song: "Wyoming"   State Tree: Cottonwood

Grand Teton National Park "Towering more than a mile above the valley of Jackson Hole, the Grand Teton rises to 13,770 feet. Twelve Teton peaks reach above 12,000 feet and support a dozen mountain glaciers…. The Teton Range is the youngest range in the Rockies and displays some of North America's oldest rocks." The National Park Service includes Yellowstone, the nation's first National Park, Devils Tower Monument, Fossil Butte National Monument, Petrified Forest, Flaming Gorge and Bighorn Canyon National Recreation Areas as protected sites. Historic sites seem unending. Western frontier history was created in Wyoming by such people as John Colter, Jim Bridger, Kit Carson, Jedediah Smith, and William F. "Buffalo Bill" Cody. Scenic Wyoming has a strong tourism base as well as mining that adds to the economic strength of the state. *Photo by Shangle Photographics*

Words of Wisdom by Great Americans

"Single acts of tyranny may be ascribed to the accidental opinion of a day; but a series of oppressions, begun at a distinguished period, and pursued unalterably through every change of ministers, too plainly proves a deliberate, systematic plan of reducing us to slavery."—*Thomas Jefferson*

"The highest glory of the American Revolution was this: it connected, in one indissoluble bond, the principles of civil government with the principles of Christianity."—*John Quincy Adams*

"The Constitution is not an instrument for the government to restrain the people, it is an instrument for the people to restrain the government—lest it come to dominate our lives and interests."—*Patrick Henry*

"An equal application of law to every condition of man is fundamental."—*Thomas Jefferson*

"I look forward to a great future for America—a future in which our country will match its military strength with our moral restraint, its wealth with our wisdom, its power with our purposes. I look forward to an America which will not be afraid of grace and beauty…which will reward achievement in business or statecraft…which commands respect throughout the world not only for its strength but for its civilization as well."—*John F. Kennedy*

95

Tragedy Unites Americans Around The Flag

By Major General Patrick Brady (U. S. Army-Retired)

The September 11 terrorist attack on the United States is testament that, tragically, it often takes tragedy to bring out the patriotism of the American people. In times of peace and prosperity the elite snicker, even scoff, at patriotism. For most of us it is present, but dormant. But in times of national heartbreak, disaster and chaos, patriotism is rampant and the people turn to patriotic symbols, especially to Old Glory, for comfort. In this uniquely horrific time we find more people buying and flying our flag than at any time since Desert Storm.

The Congress, along with millions nationwide, urges us to show our colors at home, at work and in every public place. Why? Because no other symbol unifies, comforts and inspires us quite like the red, white and blue of the Star-Spangled Banner. And there is no other symbol that more brilliantly shows our resolve to crush those who would dare to attack us.

There will be many symbolic acts in the future; memorials will be built and vigils will be held for years to come. Symbolically, Congress called on Americans to fly their flags for 30 days to "provide a physical tribute in memory of those we lost" on September 11. But we can and should do more. Protecting the flag from desecration could, more than anything else, memorialize forever those who have suffered at the hands of those who hate America. In their honor we should return to the people the right to protect Old Glory, we should pass the flag amendment.

There could be no better time. The Amendment has passed the House and enjoys the support of 80 percent of the people, perhaps more now.

Burning our flag is the most visible sign of hatred of America. And because of a mistake by our Supreme Court, flag burners are allowed to do that. We should take that away from them. In honor of those who have suffered at the hands of those who hate us, it is time to say to flag burners that we despise your hatred, we will not allow you to freely desecrate the symbol of all that is decent in the world, the symbol of our unity and of the goodness of those who were massacred.

All Americans should fly their flag as a sign of unity and resolve, not just now but always. Let's give back to all Americans a flag, as it is today, unsullied by politics and partisan bickering. Let's call on our state and federal representatives to pass the flag protection amendment as a symbol of our compassion for those who have suffered in this disaster, and as a statement of our resolve to show no mercy to those who hate us and would destroy our freedom.

Maj. Gen. Patrick Brady (USA-Ret.) is the Chairman of the Indianapolis-based Citizens Flag Alliance (CFA). The CFA is a broad-based coalition of 142 organizations committed to seeking passage of a constitutional amendment which would return to the American people the right to protect their flag. Gen. Brady was award the Medal of Honor for his service in the Vietnam War during which time he rescued over 5,000 casualties of war.

The Citizens Flag Alliance, Inc. is a coalition of organizations, most of which are national in scope, that have come together for one reason: to persuade the Congress of the United States to propose a constitutional amendment to protect the American flag from physical desecration, and send it to the states for ratification.

To contact Citizens Flag Alliance (CFA)

1. *P.O. Box 7197, Indianapolis, Indiana 46207-7197*
2. *Telephone: (317) 630-1384*
3. *Fax: (317) 630-1385*